NEW YORK
PERFORMANCE
ASSESSMENT

Approaching Common Core Assessments with Confidence

By Carol Jago

In order to get good at anything, you need to practice. Whether the goal is to improve your jump shot, level up in a video game, or make the cut in band tryouts, success requires repeated practice on the court, computer, and field. The same is true of reading and writing. The only way to get good at them is by reading and writing.

Malcolm Gladwell estimates in his book *Outliers* that mastering a skill requires about 10,000 hours of dedicated practice. He argues that individuals who are outstanding in their field have one thing in common—many, many hours of working at it. Gladwell claims that success is less dependent on innate talent than it is on practice. Now I'm pretty sure that I could put in 10,000 hours at a ballet studio and still be a terrible dancer, but I agree with Gladwell that, "Practice isn't the thing you do once you're good. It's the thing you do that makes you good."

Not just any kind of practice will help you master a skill, though. Effective practice needs to focus on improvement. That is why this series of reading and writing tasks begins with a model of the kind of reading and writing you are working towards, then takes you through practice exercises, and finally invites you to perform the skills you have practiced.

Once through the cycle is only the beginning. You will want to repeat the process many times over until close reading, supporting claims with evidence, and crafting a compelling essay is something you approach with confidence. Notice that I didn't say "with ease." I wish it were otherwise, but in my experience as a teacher and as an author, writing well is never easy.

The work is worth the effort. Like a star walking out on the stage, you put your trust in the hours you've invested in practice to result in thundering applause. To our work together!

COMMON CORE

Unit 1 Argumentative Essay
Relationships

STEP 1 ANALYZE THE MODEL

How might it be better to be at the center of one group of friends? How might it be better to be at the perimeter of several groups of friends?

Read Source Materials

STEP 2 PRACTICE THE TASK

The Debate Over Consensus Decision Making

Read Source Materials

STEP 3 PERFORM THE TASK

The Debate Over Making Friends on the Internet

Read Source Materials

Unit 2 Informative Essay
Ancient Civilizations

STEP 1 ANALYZE THE MODEL

Exploring Peru

Read Source Materials

© Houghton Mifflin Harcourt Publishing Company • Image Credits: ©Age Fotostock; ©Frank Slack/Flickr/Getty Images

STEP 2 PRACTICE THE TASK

What can you teach about the Mayan and Egyptian pyramids?

Read Source Materials

STEP 3 PERFORM THE TASK

In what ways were the Maya, the Aztecs, and the Inca advanced for their time?

Read Source Materials

Unit 3 Literary Analysis
Techniques

Unit 4 Mixed Practice
On Your Own

© Houghton Mifflin Harcourt Publishing Company

Relationships

Argumentative Essay

© Houghton Mifflin Harcourt Publishing Company

STEP 1 ANALYZE THE MODEL

Evaluate an argumentative essay that offers a position about choosing to be at the center of a small group of friends vs. being on the perimeter of several.

STEP 2 PRACTICE THE TASK

Write an argumentative essay that takes a precise position about reaching a consensus vs. disagreeing.

STEP 3 PERFORM THE TASK

Write an argumentative essay that takes a precise position about Internet friendships.

Questioning another person's point of view is something we as humans love to do. Interacting with others—friends, neighbors, relatives, strangers—sometimes can lead to disagreements. Arguing, giving your reasons for your stance on an issue, and explaining your point of view can be challenging on a person-to-person level.

The argumentative essay, on the other hand, is a more formally constructed argument.

IN THIS UNIT, you will learn how to write an argumentative essay that is based on your close reading and analysis of several relevant sources. You will learn a step-by-step approach to stating a claim and to organizing your essay to support your claim in a clear and logical way.

STEP 1

ANALYZE THE MODEL

How might it be better to be at the center of one group of friends? How might it be better to be at the perimeter of several groups of friends?

You will read:

▶ **TWO INFORMATIONAL ARTICLES**

New School, New Groups of Friends

Teen Friendships: A Cauldron of Closeness

You will analyze:

▶ **A STUDENT MODEL**
Are Close Friends Better?

The following texts were used by Ms. Jefferson's student, Philip Patel, as sources for his essay "Are Close Friends Better?" As you read, make notes in the side columns and underline information that you find useful.

NOTES

New School, New Groups of Friends

by Linda Henderson in *Washington High School Journal,* **2 December 2014, p. 5**

It was really tough moving and starting from scratch at a new school, but after a year, I can say that there have been some good things as well as bad ones.

At my old school, I was part of a small group of "band geeks." That's what we called ourselves because that's what we were. I was right at the center of the group. I helped decide things like what we were going to do for fun, where we would sit in the lunchroom, and who we would hang out with. I'm not saying we were a clique but we knew each other really well and all agreed that we didn't want a lot of random kids hanging out with us.

The problem with a group like that is that it is hard to change and try new things without your friends getting mad at you or thinking you are rejecting them. So, at my new school, I've made an effort not to get too tight with any one group, but to try new things and stay flexible. I like being involved with a few groups and getting to know kids with different interests, even if I'm not right at the center of things. It's a relief not to have to worry about any of the intense friendship drama and just have fun doing cool activities and meeting new people.

I certainly miss my old gang of friends, but it's been a lot of fun having this chance to spread myself out.

1. Analyze 2. Practice 3. Perform

Teen Friendships:
A CAULDRON OF CLOSENESS

by Gregory Buchanan in *Modern Teenagers,* March 2013, p. 18

It will come as no surprise to parents that the teenage years are particularly intense when it comes to friendships and group dynamics. Many of our children find themselves both benefitting from—and sometimes struggling with—issues relating to being part of a group of friends.

According to a 2013 study by the Adolescent Psychology Association, membership in a small, close peer group bolsters a teen's sense of identity, develops a feeling of belonging, and fosters loyal, lasting friendships. Being part of a group can mean fewer awkward social moments, fewer social decisions to make, and more social stability and security.

Problems arise when a group becomes too small, too closed and limiting, or too controlling. The teenage years are times of great change and growth, and children should be free to rethink themselves and their friendships without the limitation of what can amount to a group veto.

Being the center of a tightly knit group can mean that there is less freedom to explore, meet new friends, and try out other interests and ideas. It is important that children understand that even the best of friends sometimes grow apart. They may no longer share the same interests. It is normal, natural, and healthy to change and grow, and even sometimes grow apart.

Maintaining a variety of friendships, some close, and some more casual, can help a teen through a tough transition out of a group. Also, it is important to remind teens to conduct themselves in a manner that they will have no cause to regret later on, always being fair, upfront, and generous. People of all ages do well when they remember that being right isn't as important as being kind.

Discuss and Decide

You have read two sources about social circles. Without going any further, discuss this question: Is it better to be at the center of one group of friends or at the perimeter of several? Cite text evidence in your discussion.

Analyze a Student Model for Step 1

Read Philip's essay closely. The red side notes are the comments that his teacher, Ms. Jefferson, wrote.

Philip Patel
Ms. Jefferson
English 9
November 18

Are Close Friends Better?

Interesting hook.

Do I really have to choose? If I could have my way, I would have both. I'd be at the center of a small group of close friends, but I'd also have a wide range of more casual friendships. Being at the perimeter of a number of groups would be a good balance to my more intense and cliquish small group. I'd have depth as well as breadth, and I'd have options if anything ever went wrong in my small group.

The issue and your claim are clear.

Transition signals change in thought.

But let's say I can't have both and I have to choose one. In that case, I would choose to be at the center of a group of friends, even if that group were only three or four people. Here's why: no number of casual friends can equal the benefit of having one or two true close friends. Close friends are nothing like casual friends. You can trust them. You can laugh with them. They are there for you when life is good and when it is tough. Gregory Buchanan notes that a small group can "provide close, loyal, and lasting friendships" (18).

Valid reason, clearly stated.

Clear text citations woven into your writing.

I know the value of close friends from personal experience. Last year I was having a lot of trouble with a teacher, and my two best friends really helped me out. I don't know what I would have done without them.

Also, being at the center of something is completely different from being on the outside. When you are in the center of a small group of friends, you have a say over things. Linda Henderson says that she "helped decide things" in her small group (5). You can say what you prefer and what you really think. You can make decisions, or help make decisions. You are in charge.

1. Analyze   2. Practice   3. Perform

When you are on the perimeter of a group, you are on the outside looking in. You can decide to join in or not, but you can't really participate in decision-making, and that can get frustrating.

It is nice to know people from many different groups with many different interests. There is less pressure on individual friendships and less pressure to make decisions that might make some friends upset. You also don't get boxed in by a group that might limit your experiences (Henderson 5). But scientific studies have shown that if you end up without close friends, you'll be missing out on the ways a close-knit group can make your teenage years easier and more stable (Buchanan 18).

It's true that being at the center of a small group is like putting all your eggs in one basket. Yes, it has more risks, but it also has more rewards. There is nothing quite as special as a group of close friends.

Wide variety of evidence used, including anecdote, commonly accepted beliefs, and expert opinion.

Concluding statement restates claim and summarizes its strengths over the opposing claim.

Works Cited

Buchanan, Gregory. "Teen Friendships: A Cauldron of Closeness." *Modern Teenagers* Mar. 2013: 18. Print.

Henderson, Linda. "New School, New Groups of Friends." *Washington High School Journal* 2 Dec. 2014: 5. Print.

Discuss and Decide

Did Philip's essay convince you that it is better to have a small circle of friends?
If so, which of his reasons are the most compelling?

Terminology of Argumentative Texts

Read each term and explanation. Then look back at Philip Patel's argumentative essay and find an example to complete the chart.

Term	Explanation	Example from Philip's Essay
audience	The **audience** for your argument is a group of people that you want to convince. As you develop your argument, consider your audience's knowledge level and concerns.	
purpose	The **purpose** for writing an argument is to sway the audience. Your purpose should be clear, whether it is to persuade your audience to agree with your claim, or to motivate your audience to take some action.	
precise claim	A **precise claim** confidently states your viewpoint. Remember that you must be able to find reasons and evidence to support your claim, and that you must distinguish your claim from opposing claims.	
reason	A **reason** is a statement that supports your claim. (You should have more than one reason.) Note that you will need to supply evidence for each reason you state.	
opposing claim	An **opposing claim,** or **counterclaim**, shares the point of view of people who do not agree with your claim. Opposing claims must be fairly presented with evidence.	

PRACTICE THE TASK

The Debate Over Consensus Decision Making

You will read:

▶ **A NEWSPAPER ARTICLE**
Consensus Will Be Used to Decide School Board Policy

▶ **AN INFORMATIONAL ARTICLE**
How to Reach a Consensus

▶ **A LIST**
Is Consensus Decision-Making Right for Your Group?

▶ **TWO LETTERS TO THE EDITOR**

You will write:

▶ **AN ARGUMENTATIVE ESSAY**
Take a precise position about reaching decisions by consensus.

Source Materials for Step 2

AS YOU READ Analyze and annotate the sources in ways that help you reach a decision regarding consensus.

Source 1: Newspaper Article

Consensus Will Be Used to Decide School Board Policy

by Soledad Stephens, Education Correspondent   **May 25, 2012**

At a meeting last night, the Tiberi Township School Board chose a new method to determine standards for grade promotion. Normally the 12-person board votes on the proposals. Now they will use consensus to build a plan of action acceptable to all. Although none are likely to get their first choice, there will also be no winners and no losers.

Consensus decision-making is very different from voting. Voting is a way to choose between alternatives. With consensus, a group can bring the best parts of many proposals together to create something new. Voting is faster, but it may leave some "defeated" voters upset with the outcome. When a group achieves consensus after a thorough discussion, all parties are on board with the outcome.

"I'm just pleased we will be working together to shape a proposal that everyone can get behind," said School Board President Patti Rincon.

However, not all are in consensus about using consensus.

"Consensus is too much compromise," said parent Tyrell Washington. "Everyone gives up something and no one really likes the final result. They should keep working until they have a proposal that everyone likes, unanimously!"

School administrator Jesse VanDeLaar thinks just the opposite. "These decisions should be made by the experts," he declared. "It really isn't useful to vote or reach consensus. This is not a popularity contest—it's a question of what the research has shown will or will not work."

Good luck to the members of the school board on reaching a consensus that will be accepted by all stakeholders—parents, teachers, *and* school administrators.

Tiberi Times, Harding, New York, p. 3

1. Analyze   2. Practice   3. Perform

How to Reach a Consensus

From "How to Make Group Decisions." *Group Dynamics.* **Organizational Media Group, undated, Web. Retrieved Feb. 18, 2014.**

A *consensus* is when a group of people reaches a general agreement. Getting to a consensus requires a special decision-making process that takes everyone's opinions and concerns into account. In consensus decision-making, everyone is included, everyone participates, everyone's voice is equal, and everyone works towards the same goal—finding a solution.

1. Define and describe the issue that needs to be decided.

2. Decide how your group will reach a final decision. (Some groups insist on unanimity; others accept a consensus with one or two dissenting voices.)

3. List all the concerns that the final proposal should address.

4. Brainstorm and record a list of possible solutions. Encourage every participant to offer ideas, opinions, and comments.

5. Evaluate the list of alternatives. Write up a draft proposal that combines the best of all the ideas.

6. Revise the proposal until it best meets the interests of the group.

Close Read

You've read two sources on reaching a consensus. Explain some advantages to making decisions this way, and cite text evidence to support your response.

_____

_____

Is Consensus Decision-Making Right for Your Group?

From *Working in Groups* by James Anderson, Wilson Publishing, New York, 2011, p. 113

Advantages of Consensus Decision-Making:

▶ Consensus decision-making helps build trust and a sense of community.

▶ Everyone's ideas are included, which leads to a wider range of possible solutions.

▶ The solutions are supported by the whole group.

Reaching a consensus may be difficult if:

▶ the group has not worked together before or is too large (15 or more).

▶ some members do not understand or accept the consensus-seeking process, or argue, bully, or intimidate others.

▶ the issue is complicated with few viable solutions available.

▶ one member has more power than others (this may discourage others from speaking freely).

▶ there is a lack of trust among group members.

▶ there is not enough time for discussion.

▶ group leaders try to control outcomes rather than facilitate discussion.

▶ one or two "dissenters" hold up the whole process.

▶ there is no agreed-upon consensus process for the group to use.

Discuss and Decide

When might making a decision by consensus not be the best method to use?

1. Analyze   2. Practice   3. Perform

Source 4: Letters to the Editor

To the Editor

I'm writing to protest the School Board's recent adoption of the consensus decision-making method to decide grade promotion policy. This is not a situation where it is appropriate to choose a course of action by finding something that everyone can agree on. Maybe everyone agrees on a plan that makes no sense at all. Decisions about grade promotions should be made by administrators who have responsibility and experts who have special knowledge. We owe our students the BEST decisions, not just the most popular ones.

Yours truly,
Jesse VanDeLaar
Deputy Principal

Tiberi Times, **Harding, New York, May 30, 2012, p. 12**

To the Editor

Congratulations to the School Board for choosing to make their policy decisions by consensus! No longer will the policies they adopt be the subject of bitter disagreements and lackluster support. We parents will no longer feel like cats who have left the mice to play. When the whole school board unites behind a plan, then teachers, parents, and students will unite behind it as well. A plan which has taken into consideration the opinions and interests of all the members—and survived extensive debate—is a plan that will stand the test of time.

In a world with far too much strife and conflict, few leaders seem to have the skills needed to compromise and work together effectively. Hats off to the school board for leading by example.

Mary Anne Dunlop
Parent

Discuss and Decide

Which claims in one letter are not directly refuted in the other letter?

Respond to Questions on Step 2 Sources

These questions will help you analyze the sources you've read. Use your notes and refer back to the sources in order to answer the questions. Your answers to these questions will help you write your essay.

1 Evaluate the sources. Is the evidence from one source more credible than the evidence from another source? When you evaluate the credibility of a source, examine the expertise of the author and/or the organization responsible for the information. Record your reasons in the chart.

Source	Credible?	Reasons
Newspaper Article Consensus Will Be Used to Decide School Board Policy		
Informational Article How to Reach a Consensus		
List Is Consensus Decision-Making Right for Your Group?		
Letters to the Editor		

2 **Prose Constructed-Response** If you disagreed with Mary Anne Dunlop's position on decision-making by consensus, which sources would you use to refute her argument? Why?

_____

_____

3 **Prose Constructed-Response** Which source best complements the information found in the list, "Is Consensus Decision-Making Right for Your Group?" Explain your rationale, citing evidence from the text.

_____

_____

Searching for Evidence

Every reason you offer to support the central claim of your argument must be upheld by evidence. It is useful to think ahead about evidence when you are preparing to write an argument. If there is no evidence to support your claim, you will need to revise your claim. The evidence you provide must be relevant, or related to your claim. It must also be sufficient. Sufficient evidence is both clear and varied. Using evidence from several different sources shows the prominence of the issue and your idea about it. If evidence is pulled from only one source, it calls the credibility of the argument into question.

Use this chart to help you vary the types of evidence you provide to support your reasons.

Types of Evidence	What Does It Look Like?
Anecdotes: personal examples or stories that illustrate a point	
Commonly accepted beliefs: ideas that most people share	
Examples: specific instances or illustrations of a general idea	
Expert opinion: statement made by an authority on the subject	
Facts: statements that can be proven true, such as statistics or other numerical information	

Write an argumentative essay that takes a precise position about reaching decisions by consensus.

Planning and Prewriting

Before you draft your essay, complete some important planning steps.

Claim ➡ Reasons ➡ Evidence

 You may prefer to do your planning on a computer.

Make a Precise Claim

1. Is reaching consensus always a good idea? Are there times when it is better to disagree?

2. Review the evidence on pages 10–13. Do the sources support your position?

3. If you answered *no* to Question 2, you can either change your position or do additional research to find supporting evidence.

4. State your claim. It should be precise. It should contain the issue and your position on the issue.

Issue: Decision-making by consensus

Your position on the issue: _____

Your precise claim: _____

State Reasons

Next, gather support for your claim. Identify several valid reasons that justify your position.

Reason 1	Reason 2	Reason 3

Find Evidence

You have identified reasons that support your claim. Summarize your reasons in the chart below. Then complete the chart by identifying evidence that supports your reasons.

Relevant Evidence: The evidence you plan to use must be *relevant* to your argument. That is, it should directly and factually support your position.

Sufficient Evidence: Additionally, your evidence must be *sufficient* to make your case. That is, you need to supply enough evidence to convince others.

Varied Evidence: Finally, be sure your evidence is *varied*. It should come from multiple sources and represent different types of evidence—anecdote, commonly accepted beliefs, examples, expert opinion, and/or facts.

Short Summary of Reasons	Evidence
Reason 1	Relevant? _____ Sufficient? _____ Varied? _____
Reason 2	Relevant? _____ Sufficient? _____ Varied? _____
Reason 3	Relevant? _____ Sufficient? _____ Varied? _____

Address Opposing Claims

You have written out your precise claim, reasons that you support it, and evidence that supports those reasons. Now you need to anticipate opposing claims and address them so that your argument is the most persuasive. Remember that there is an opposing claim for every argument, no matter how strong.

Once you've identified an opposing claim, select one or more ways to refute it. These include:

▶ Challenging the credibility of the source supporting the opposing claim

▶ Noting that the opposing claim is true only in certain circumstances

▶ Noting that the opposing claim addresses only certain facts, not all facts

▶ Explaining the possible biases influencing the opposing claim

Follow these steps:

Task	Arguments
Identify the Opposing Claim(s) Review your precise claim. Then review your source material to find claims that oppose yours. Write out one or more of these opposing claims clearly.	
Select Ways to Refute the Opposing Claim(s) Think carefully about each opposing claim. Is it: • credible? • true in certain circumstances only? • based on a complete set of facts? • biased? Write notes on the best way to refute the claim.	

1. Analyze   2. Practice   3. Perform

Finalize Your Plan

Whether you are writing your essay at home or working in a timed situation at school, it is important to have a plan. You will save time and create a more organized, logical essay by planning the structure before you start writing.

Use your responses on pages 16–18, as well as your close reading notes, to complete the graphic organizer.

▶ Think about how you will grab your reader's attention with an interesting fact or anecdote.

▶ State your precise claim.

▶ Identify the issue and your position.

▶ List the likely opposing claim and how you will counter it.

▶ Restate your claim.

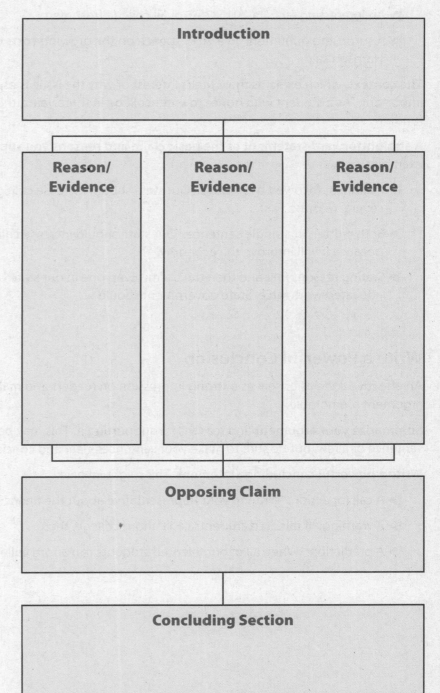

Write a Clear and Engaging Introduction

An effective introduction includes:

A hook that engages readers and grabs their attention. Some examples:

> ▶ A rhetorical question: "What if college were so cheap that everyone could go?"

> ▶ An anecdote: "When my grandfather began college in 1965, . . ."

> ▶ An interesting fact: "In 2015, 75% of all college freshmen . . ."

> ▶ A surprising quotation: "In a 2015 speech on the growing costs of college, Senator Harrison said . . ."

The context, which explains the writer's interest or why the issue is especially important: "As a student who hopes to enter college in three years, the recent cut in funding . . ."

A straightforward statement of the basic claim and reasons you support it. Some examples:

> ▶ Claim first followed by reasons: "Our state should increase college financial aid for several reasons. First, . . ."

> ▶ Both written in a single sentence: "Our state should increase college financial aid because it will improve the economy."

> ▶ Stating reasons first and then the claim: "Everyone in our state benefits from an educated work force. State government should . . ."

Write a Powerful Conclusion

An effective conclusion leaves a strong impression on readers and makes your argument memorable.

Summarize your argument and reasons for supporting it. This may be a single sentence or a few, but be sure to make your sentences clear and concise.

Write a powerful concluding statement. This might involve:

> ▶ A call for action: "Write to your Representative about the financial aid bill . . ."

> ▶ A warning: "If talented students can't afford college, then . . ."

> ▶ A prediction: "When all of our talented students can afford college, our state will . . ."

Cite Your Sources

A credible argumentative essay is based on reliable sources that are cited within the essay and listed at the end. Many teachers and organizations support the format used by the Modern Language Association (MLA). This style is used in the sample essay on pages 6–7.

Create a "Works Cited" List

Place Citations within Your Essay Be sure to include citations in your essay each time you use a direct quote or an important piece of background information. If the author's name appears in the same sentence, include just the page number in parentheses right before the ending punctuation. If the author's name doesn't appear in the sentence, list the author's last name before the page number.

Getting Help Online As with many other modern tasks, there is software that can help you create correct citations within your essay and list the sources at the end. If you have Internet access, several options are available at http://mlaformat.org/mla-format-generator/. It is always best to understand the process and guidelines, whether you use an online generator or complete the process on your own. Follow the steps below to learn about the process and complete essential tasks.

Make Notes on Each Source You'll need the following information to create citations with a generator or to complete them yourself (information for websites and print sources differs slightly):

▶ Author(s)
▶ Publication title and type of publication (newspaper, book, website, etc.)
▶ Publisher
▶ Date of publication
▶ Page numbers, especially if there are multiple pages, if you are quoting directly from the publication, or if you are using specific rather than general information, such as statistics or dates

Create Your "Works Cited" List Use the following bulleted suggestions to format and perfect your list:

▶ List all of the sources you have used in your essay on the Works Cited list.
▶ The author is always listed with the last name first. The list is then arranged by alphabetical order of the first word in each entry (usually the author's last name).
▶ Check with your teacher to see if he or she would like the actual Web address (URL) for an Internet source to appear in the citation. (The MLA no longer requires it.)
▶ Use these guidelines for creating your Works Cited list for the sources on pages 10–13:

  Newspaper: Author(s). "Title of Article." *Title of Periodical* Day Month Year: pages. Medium of publication.

  Website: Editor, author, or compiler name (if available). *Name of Site.* Version number. Name of institution/organization affiliated with the site (sponsor or publisher), date of resource creation (if available). Medium of publication. Date of access.

  Book: Author(s). *Title of Book.* City of publication: Publisher, Year of publication. Medium of publication.

Draft Your Essay

As you write, think about:

▶ **Audience:** Your teacher and classmates

▶ **Purpose:** Demonstrate your understanding of the specific requirements of an argumentative essay.

▶ **Style:** Use a formal and objective tone that isn't defensive.

▶ **Transitions:** Use words such as *furthermore, consequently, nevertheless,* or *on the contrary* to create cohesion or flow.

Revise

Revision Checklist: Self Evaluation

Use the checklist below to guide your analysis.

 If you drafted your essay on the computer, you may wish to print it out so that you can more easily evaluate it.

Ask Yourself	Tips	Revision Strategies
Does the introduction grab the audience's attention and include a precise claim?	Draw a wavy line under the attention-grabbing text. Bracket the claim.	Add an attention grabber. Check that the order you use to state the claim and supporting reasons is the most convincing. Combine sentences for a smoother introduction.
Do at least two valid reasons support the claim? Is each reason supported by relevant and sufficient evidence?	Underline each reason. Circle each piece of evidence, and draw an arrow to the reason it supports.	Add reasons or revise existing ones to make them more valid. Add relevant evidence to ensure that your support is sufficient.
Do transitions create cohesion and link parts of the argument?	Put a star next to each transition.	Add words, phrases, or clauses to connect related ideas so writing flows smoothly.
Are the reasons presented in an order and with transitions that help you to sound convincing? Are connections clear?	Number the reasons in the margin, ranking them by their strength and effectiveness.	Rearrange the reasons into a more logical order of importance.
Are opposing claims fairly addressed, discussed, and refuted?	Circle any sentence that addresses an opposing claim.	Add sentences that identify and address those opposing claims.
Does the concluding section restate the claim, summarize key points, and include a warning, prediction, or call for action?	Put a box around the restatement of your claim.	Add a sentence that restates your claim.
Have you cited all your sources correctly?	Highlight all the information that comes from another source.	Use MLA format to add sources in parentheses and in your Works Cited list.

Revision Checklist: Peer Review

Exchange your essay with a classmate, or read it aloud to your partner. As you read and comment on your classmate's essay, focus on logic, organization, and evidence—not on whether you agree with the author's claim. Help each other identify parts of the draft that need strengthening, reworking, or a new approach.

What To Look For	Notes for My Partner
Does the introduction contain an attention grabber and include the claim and supporting reasons arranged in a clear, convincing manner?	
Do at least two valid reasons support the claim? Is each reason supported by relevant and sufficient evidence?	
Do transitions and the precise use of vocabulary words help connect ideas and link related parts of the essay?	
Are the reasons stated in body paragraphs valid, mindful of counterclaims, sufficient, and arranged in the most persuasive manner possible?	
Are opposing claims fairly acknowledged and refuted?	
Does the concluding section restate the claim, summarize major points, and possibly include a warning, a prediction, or a call for action?	
Are all sources cited in the correct format?	

Edit

 Edit your essay to correct spelling, grammar, and punctuation errors.

NOTES

The Debate Over Making Friends on the Internet

You will read:

▶ **A NEWSPAPER ARTICLE**
Study: The Internet Helps You Make More Friends, Be More Social

▶ **A BLOG**
Social Media, Pretend Friends, and the Lie of False Intimacy

▶ **A MAGAZINE ARTICLE**
Making Friends Through the Internet

You will write:

▶ **AN ARGUMENTATIVE ESSAY**
Take a precise position regarding Internet friendships.

Part 1: Read Sources

Source 1: Newspaper Article

Study:
The Internet Helps You Make More Friends, Be More Social

by Graeme McMillan, from *Time*, www.techland.time.com, June 16, 2011

AS YOU READ *Analyze the data presented in the articles. Look for evidence that supports your position regarding online friendships or inspires you to change your position.*

NOTES

It's the kind of news you can use next time concerned parents bring up the idea that the internet is making people more withdrawn and closed off from the rest of humanity: A new study from the Pew Research Center has found that online social networks actually seem to make people more social.

Pew polled 2,255 Americans during October and November last year, and of the 1,787 internet users in that group, 47% used social networking sites. Facebook was used by 92% of the 975 people that used social networks, with MySpace in second place, with 29%.

10 Linkedin and Twitter trailed behind, with 18% and 13% respectively.

That's almost twice as many as in 2008, when the survey was last held. But more interestingly, there's also been a rise in the number of close friendships people are reporting when compared with 2008—2.16 close friends on average, compared with 2008's 1.93—with that increase being lead by those online, who reported an average of 2.26 close friends to the offline respondents' 1.75. It gets even better when you look at those using social networks, who reported 2.45 close friends on average.

Discuss and Decide

The author includes information about the number of close friends reported. What trend does the Pew survey seem to reveal? Cite text evidence in your discussion.

1. Analyze   2. Practice   3. Perform

> ***"** …online Americans tend to have 664 [social] ties on average, compared with an offline average of around 506. **"***

The study even looked into the number of social ties internet
20   users and non-internet users have, and found that online Americans
tend to have 664 ties on average, compared with an offline average
of around 506. That number goes crazy when you start to plug in
different social networks, however: Facebook users average 648 social
ties, but Twitter users have an average of 838.

So, the next time someone says that they think the internet is bad
for society, the answer is clear: Sign them up for Twitter, and see how
they feel a couple of weeks later.

Close Read

1. How did Pew Research collect their data?

_____

_____

2. Explain the change in the number of people using social networking sites
from 2008 to 2011.

_____

_____

3. Are the increases in "close friends" and "ties" similar or different? Cite
evidence from the text to support your answer.

_____

_____

_____

Social Media, Pretend Friends, and the Lie of False Intimacy

by Jay Baer from *Convince & Convert* website (Convince & Convert, LLC)

AS YOU READ *How is this information shaping your position regarding online friendships?*

NOTES

It's not an illusion. We really are doing more with each 24 hours, as technology enables (or forces) us to interact and intersect and do and consume with unprecedented volume and vigor. **We live our lives at breakneck speed because we can, because we feel we have to keep up, and because every macro and micro breeze blows in that direction.**

I remember the days before social media when I would get 20 phone calls per day and 50 or 60 emails, and felt exhausted by the pace of communication. Now we've traded the telephone for other

10 connection points (I only get 2-3 calls per day), but the overall number of people ringing our doorbell through some mechanism has ballooned like Charles Barkley.

The number of "inboxes" we possess is staggering: Email (3 accounts for me), public Twitter, Twitter DM, public Facebook, Facebook messages, Facebook chat, Linkedin messages, public Google +, Google + messages, blog comments, Skype, text messages, Instagram, phone, voice mail, and several topically or geographically specific forums, groups and social networks. That's a lot of relationship bait in the water.

Close Read

How does the blogger use diction and rhetorical devices (including formatting and text features) to let us know his position regarding online friendships? What inferences does he encourage us to make? How?

_____

_____

1. Analyze   2. Practice   3. Perform

The Lie of Opportunity

20 How do we justify this? How do we convince ourselves that slicing our attention so thin the turkey becomes translucent is a good idea?

We do it because we believe that more relationships provide more opportunity.

"It's not what you know, it's who you know."

"Social media makes a big world smaller."

"Linkedin is for people you know, Facebook is for people you used to know, Twitter is for people you want to know."

All of these chestnuts are passed around like a flu strain
30 because they make intuitive sense. But common among them is the **underlying premise that interacting with more people is inherently better than interacting with fewer people.** I have always believed this to be true, and in fact have delivered the lines above in presentations and on this blog. But today, I'm no longer convinced.

Instead I wonder, what if we have it ALL wrong?

I recognize this is not purely an either/or scenario, and relationships that began with a Twitter exchange or series of blog comments can flourish into treasured real-world ties.

But those situations where we "meet" someone through social
40 media, have the opportunity to interact in real life, and then develop a relationship that creates true friendship are few and far between. **And as social media gets bigger and more pervasive, this chasm becomes even more difficult to cross.** As my own networks in social media have gotten larger, I've ended up talking about my personal life less, because a large percentage of that group don't know me, or my wife, or my kids, or my town, or my interests. I don't want to bore people with the inanities of the everyday. (Facebook is the one exception, as I've always kept my personal account relatively small).

To some degree, I think this explains the popularity of Google +
50 among people with very large followings on Twitter and/or Facebook. Google + provides a chance for a do-over, to create a new group of connections that are more carefully cultivated.

NOTES

But that's just medicating the symptoms, not curing the disease. **Fundamentally, technology and our use of it isn't—as we've all hoped—bringing us closer together.** In fact, it may be driving us farther apart, as we know more and more people, but know less and less about each of them.

Making Friends Out of Connections

Maybe we should be focused less on making a lot of connections, and focused more on making a few real friends? I'm
60 going to try to work on this, to identify people with whom I want to develop real friendships, and make a concerted effort to do so, even if it means answering fewer tweets and blog comments from a much larger group of casual connections.

We have to take at least some of these social media spawned relationships to the next level, otherwise what's the point beyond generating clicks and newsletter subscribers?

You think you know someone, but you don't. And that's social media's fault. But more so, our own.

Close Read

What claim and counterclaim about the value of Internet contacts does the blogger make? Be sure to cite textual evidence in your response.

_____

_____

_____

1. Analyze   2. Practice   3. Perform

Making Friends Through the Internet
Advantages and disadvantages of meeting friends online
by Sally Arthur, *Teen Scene Magazine,* March 2015, page 16

Meeting friends on the Internet can have its advantages and disadvantages. There are a number of factors to consider.

Meeting friends online can happen more quickly than it might happen offline. You can even become friends with someone who lives in a different part of the world.

You can remain anonymous on the Internet. You do not have to share information about where you live, how old you are, or any personal details about your life. Online, you can be whoever you want to be, or just be yourself. This allows people to practice their
10 social skills in an anonymous setting.

One major disadvantage of making friends online is that you do not always know if people are who they say they are. Just as it can be a good thing to be anonymous to protect your safety and personal information, anonymity can be dangerous, too. If you are dealing with someone who is not forthcoming about their identity, you don't know his or her motive for doing so.

Making friends online also may prevent people from socializing outside of the Internet. While having friends online is a good way to find people with similar interests, friends who exist only on a
20 computer screen do not provide the companionship necessary to sustain friendships. If having Internet friends comes at the cost of neglecting friends offline, the Internet becomes a disadvantage.

While there are advantages and disadvantages to meeting friends online, it is up to every individual to use discretion and be safe.

NOTES

Discuss and Decide

Reviewing the advantages and disadvantages Arthur lists, do you have a sense of her bias? Explain your thinking, citing evidence from the text.

Respond to Questions on Step 3 Sources

These questions will help you analyze the sources you've read. Use your notes and refer back to the sources to answer the questions. Your answers to these questions will help you write your essay.

1 Is the evidence from one source more credible than the evidence from another source? When you evaluate the credibility of a source, examine the expertise of the author and/or the organization responsible for the information. Record your reasons.

Source	Credible?	Reasons
Newspaper Article Study: The Internet Helps You Make More Friends, Be More Social		
Blog Social Media, Pretend Friends, and the Lie of False Intimacy		
Magazine Article Making Friends Through the Internet		

2 **Prose Constructed-Response** What point about making friends online is raised in all three sources? Why is this point important to address when making an informed decision about the validity of online friendships? Support your answer with details and evidence.

_____

_____

_____

3 **Prose Constructed-Response** Does the evidence in "Making Friends Through the Internet" support or contradict the evidence in "Study: The Internet Helps You Make More Friends, Be More Social"? Use details from the article to support your answer.

_____

_____

_____

Part 2: Write

ASSIGNMENT

You have read about making friends online. Now write an argumentative essay in which you take a precise position about Internet friendships. Support your claim with details from what you have read.

Plan

Use the graphic organizer to help you outline the structure of your argumentative essay.

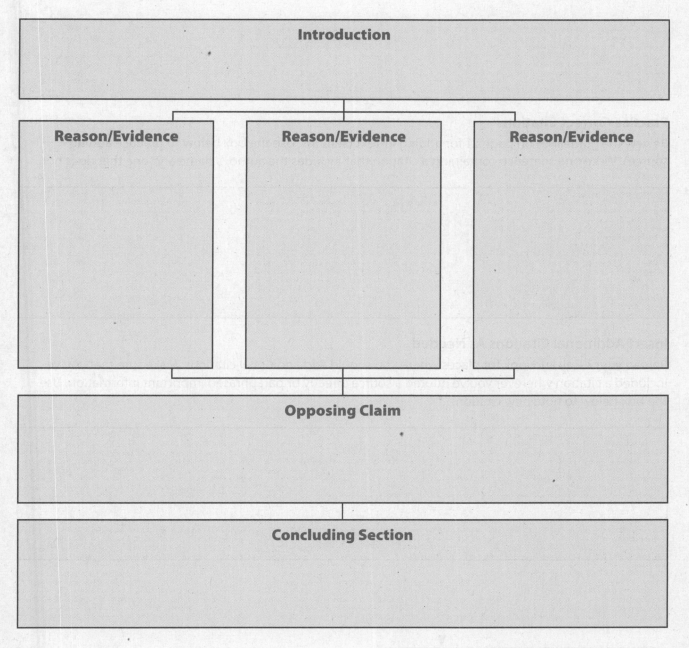

Introduction

Reason/Evidence   Reason/Evidence   Reason/Evidence

Opposing Claim

Concluding Section

Cite Additional Sources

Citing your sources is essential to a strong argumentative essay. If your essay does not contain several citations, revise it to include more. This will give readers a chance to judge the reliability of your sources and how well they support your precise position. Review the information you learned on page 21 and put it into practice below.

Create Your Works Cited List

If you haven't done it already, use the box below to list the sources on pages 26–31 in MLA format.

Practice Correct Citations

Review the guidelines on page 21 for adding in-text citations. Use the box below to practice adding sources. Write one sentence containing a citation that includes the author's name and one that does not.

Insert Additional Citations As Needed

Reread your essay and look for places where you should add additional citations. Make sure that you've included a citation wherever you've quoted a source directly or paraphrased important information. Use the box below to note new citations.

Draft

 Use your notes and completed graphic organizer to write a first draft of your argumentative essay.

Revise and Edit

 Look back over your essay and compare it to the Evaluation Criteria. Revise your essay and edit it to correct spelling, grammar, and punctuation errors.

Evaluation Criteria

Your teacher will be looking for:

1. *Statement of purpose*

▶ Is your claim specific?

▶ Did you support it with valid reasons?

▶ Did you anticipate and address opposing claims fairly?

2. *Organization*

▶ Are the sections of your essay organized in a logical way?

▶ Is there a smooth flow from beginning to end?

▶ Is there a clear conclusion that supports the argument?

▶ Did you stay on topic?

3. *Elaboration of evidence*

▶ Is the evidence relative to the topic?

▶ Is there enough evidence to be convincing?

▶ Did you cite all of your sources using a proper format?

4. *Language and vocabulary*

▶ Did you use a formal, non-combative tone?

▶ Did you use vocabulary familiar to your audience?

5. *Conventions*

▶ Did you follow the rules of grammar usage as well as punctuation, capitalization, and spelling?

▶ Did you cite all your sources, both in the text of your essay and in a Works Cited list, using the correct MLA formats?

NOTES

Ancient Civilizations

Informative Essay

ANALYZE THE MODEL

Evaluate informative essays on Cuzco, Peru and Machu Picchu.

PRACTICE THE TASK

Write an informative essay on the Mayan and Egyptian pyramids.

PERFORM THE TASK

Write an informative essay about the successes of the Maya, the Aztecs, and the Inca.

An informative essay, also called an expository essay, is a short work of nonfiction that informs and explains. Unlike fiction, nonfiction is mainly written to convey factual information, although writers of nonfiction shape information in a way that matches their own purposes. Nonfiction writing can be found in newspaper, magazine, and online articles, as well as in biographies, speeches, movie and book reviews, and true-life adventure stories.

The nonfiction topics that you will read about in this unit discuss real facts and events about ancient civilizations and structures.

IN THIS UNIT, you will analyze information from nonfiction articles, graphics, and data displays. You will study a variety of text structures that are frequently used in the writing of informative text. You will use these text structures to plan and write your essays.

ANALYZE THE MODEL

Exploring Peru

You will read:

▶ **AN INSTRUCTIONAL ARTICLE**
Chart a Course That Works!

You will analyze:

▶ **TWO STUDENT MODELS**
Cuzco, Peru

Machu Picchu: Still a Mystery

Source Materials for Step 1

Ms. Margolis's students read the article below to help them learn strategies for structuring informative essays. As you read, underline information that you find useful.

Chart a Course That Works!

You probably have already had tough writing assignments that required you to plan, research, and write an informative essay. Whether the subject is science, history, or another nonfiction topic, you should decide in advance how you will structure your essay. What do I mean by structure? A structure is a system in which all the parts have a function. When you write an informative essay, each part should support your message. Graphic organizers can help you plan your organizational structure.

Central Idea/Sub-topics/Supporting Details

The purpose of any informative essay is to give your readers more information about a topic. This is true if you are explaining a topic or describing a process. One approach is a topical structure. Use a graphic organizer like the one below if you choose this organizational style. It will help you establish your central idea, the sub-topics you will explore, and details or descriptions that support them.

Begin by jotting down a sentence that states your central idea. You may need to do some preliminary research to define your central idea. You can then identify the essential sub-topics that will give your readers the information they need to understand the central idea. Each sub-topic will be supported by details that illustrate or support the sub-topic and the central idea.

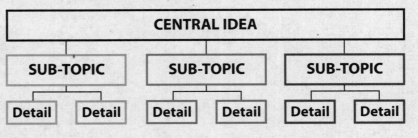

1. Analyze   2. Practice   3. Perform

Identify Sub-topics

As you plan your essay, identify the sub-topics you'll need to develop your central idea. Your sub-topics should explain or describe the central idea, but remember: an informative essay isn't a full research paper. You must limit your sub-topics to fit within your format. The example below shows how several possible sub-topics were selected to develop the central idea.

Central Idea
Los Angeles depends on water from a long distance away to survive and grow.

Possible Sub-topics					
Climate and Rainfall	~~Native Cultures~~	**Early Water Supply**	~~European Settlements~~	~~Bringing in Water~~	**Growing Water Needs**

Not closely related to central idea (arrow pointing to Native Cultures)

Research info and sub-topic similar to Early Water Supply – Combine under Early Water Supply (arrows pointing to Early Water Supply and European Settlements)

Research info more easily covered under Water Needs (arrows pointing to Bringing in Water and Growing Water Needs)

Find and Develop Supporting Details

Each sub-topic needs supporting details. An interesting informative essay uses a variety of detail types. The chart shows several types of supporting details and examples.

Supporting Details	Sub-topics and Examples
Anecdotes	**Early water supply:** The early settlers, called "Los Pobladores," find cattle dead from drought.
Commonly accepted beliefs	**Climate and rainfall:** Incorrect belief that Los Angeles has a warm climate, but isn't really a desert.
Examples	**Early water supply:** Colonists dug ditches called "zanjas" to bring water to settlement.
Expert opinions	**Growth and water supply:** Official from CA State Water Project: "LA must invest millions in water supply to continue growth."
Facts	**Climate and rainfall:** NOAA: LA average annual rainfall is 12". Houston has 50", Baltimore 40". Definition of "arid land" is 10" to 20" yearly.

Discuss and Decide

Why is it important to do preliminary research and establish a central idea before making a plan for an essay?

Analyze Two Student Models for Step 1

Ken structured his informative essay topically, with the central idea first, followed by sub-topics and and the relevant details that support them. Under each sub-topic box in his model, Ken added a box containing supporting details. (You may also want to modify your graphic organizer to meet your needs.) Read Ken's essay closely. His teacher, Ms. Margolis, wrote the red side comments.

Ken's Model

CENTRAL IDEA
Cuzco is a unique city.

History	Architecture	Food	Festivals	Prestigious Awards
Facts: Killki, Inca, Spanish	Examples: Inca, Spanish	Examples: "cuy", alpaca, lucuma	Examples: Carnival, Señor de los Temblores, Corpus Christi	Expert opinion: archaeological capital of the Americas Fact: UNESCO Heritage site

Ken Norris
Ms. Margolis, English
March 15

Cuzco, Peru

Nice factual introduction, and good use of a map.

In southeastern Peru, nestled in the towering Andes mountain range at a height of 11,200 feet above sea level, is one of the most amazing cities in the world. That city is Cuzco (ko͞o′sko͞), or *Qosqo* as it was called by the ancient Incans. In their language, the name means "navel of the earth" ("Cuzco").

History

Perhaps the most amazing thing about Cuzco is its history. The city is said to be one of the oldest inhabited developments in the Americas. The earliest inhabitants were the Killki; their culture was dominant in the area for over a thousand years.

The Inca were the next important group in the area. Their civilization began in the 12th century, and by the early 1400s the Inca Empire began to expand very quickly ("Inca"). Sometime around 1450, the Inca ruler Pachacutec developed Cuzco into the capital of the empire. Many buildings were built on Killki foundations. The city was designed in the shape of a puma, and two rivers were diverted with canals to prevent flooding. By 1500, Cuzco was one of the richest and most important cities in the Americas (Burke 92).

But then something new happened on the continent. Spanish conquistadors arrived. The Inca were involved in civil war, many fell victim to European diseases, and their warriors were no match for Spanish armored horseback cavalry. In 1533, a Spanish force of just 180 men under Francisco Pizarro took the city. Three years later, a force of between 10,000 and 100,000 Inca tried unsuccessfully to reclaim it. Cuzco remained under Spanish rule until 1821, when Peru declared independence ("Cuzco").

Architecture

One of the results of the Spanish conquest was the remarkable mix of architecture in Cuzco. The Inca stonework and precious metals were like nothing Spaniards had ever seen. Great blocks of stone were so accurately cut that there was no need for mortar. One such block that remains as part of a wall weighs over 30 tons. The

Your headings make it easy for readers to identify your sub-topics.

Interesting fact about the Killki, but it needs a citation.

Your History sub-topic is well developed with lots of interesting facts.

I like the way you've incorporated a drawing! It really brings the subject matter to life.

Spanish took the precious metals, including 700 gold panels from the Qorikancha temple that each weighed nearly five pounds. They destroyed the Inca's religious and political buildings, but built their own churches and palaces on the Inca foundations. The city retains its Inca layout and numerous examples of both Inca stonework and Spanish baroque architecture (Cameron 32).

Food

A modern visitor to Cuzco will delight in its unique and historic foods. *Cuy* is a traditional dish made from roasted guinea pig, often served whole on a plate, including its head. Like buffalo in the American West, alpaca meat in Peru makes excellent dried jerky. If you have a sweet tooth, *lucuma* is similar to mango and is used in many soft drinks and desserts ("Top 10 Things to Eat in Peru").

Awards

For these and many other reasons, Cuzco is a most amazing city. It is no wonder that it has been called the archaeological capital of the Americas (Cameron 32). It has also been named to UNESCO's Cultural Heritage List, and is a World Heritage Site. These recognitions are intended to help countries around

Festivals
Tourists can join in a variety of celebrations in Cuzco. Many show how Christianity blended with native culture over the centuries (Weston).
Carnival echoes festivals around the world and includes colorful dance competitions.
Señor de los Temblores celebrates native culture and its survival when an earthquake struck the area in 1650. Christian icons were believed to help stop the destruction.
Corpus Christi, celebrated 60 days after Easter, shows how traditional celebrations adapted to Christian feasts (Weston).

Very interesting to learn how the Spanish and Incan influences both remain in the city.

The sidebar about festivals gives information efficiently.

the world preserve unique places that illustrate the incredible accomplishments of ancient civilizations ("Frequently Asked Questions").

Cuzco is clearly a unique and fascinating place. It shows how cultures have blended over time. In Cuzco, both the Inca and the Spanish literally built on top of the architectural structures of the previous civilization.

Clear conclusion restates that Cuzco has both Inca and Spanish influences.

Works Cited

Burke, Winston. *The History of Peru*. New York: Oak Tree Publishing, 2010. Print.

Cameron, Renata. "Traveling in Peru." *World Travel*. 15 Apr. 2011: 32–36. Print.

"Cuzco." *Encyclopædia Britannica. Encyclopædia Britannica Online*. Encyclopædia Britannica Inc., 2015. Web. 6 Mar. 2015.

"Frequently Asked Questions." *UNESCO World Heritage Centre*. United Nations Educational, Scientific, and Cultural Organization, 2015. Web. 8 Mar. 2015.

"Inca." *Encyclopædia Britannica. Encyclopædia Britannica Online*. Encyclopædia Britannica Inc., 2015. Web. 6 Mar. 2015.

"Top 10 Things to Eat in Peru." *National Geographic Travel*. National Geographic Society, n.d. Web. 9 Mar. 2015.

Weston, Mike. "A Guide to the Culture and Traditions of the Andean Communities of Peru." *My Peru*. Peru Treks, 2007. Web. 8 Mar. 2015.

Your Works Cited list looks good. All the crucial information is here, and it's correctly formatted.

Discuss and Decide

How is the writing model that Ken jotted down before beginning reflected in the organization of his essay?

Claudia also chose to use a topical structure for her informative essay about Machu Picchu. She organized her essay around some of the debates concerning the reason it was built, the reason it was abandoned, and who "discovered" it.

Claudia's Model

CENTRAL IDEA
Machu Picchu is an ancient site that still puzzles historians.

SUB-TOPICS AND SUPPORTING DETAILS

Why Was It Built?
Expert Opinions: royal city; religious site, fortress
Facts: close to other sacred areas

Why Was It Abandoned?
Facts: constructed in 15th century, abandoned 100 yrs. later; Spanish never came
Expert Opinions: smallpox epidemic, drought

Who Discovered It?
Anecdotes: Bingham travel, books, etc.
Commonly held beliefs: site "discovered" but well-known to local people, and others
Expert Opinions: others came during 1800s

Why Preserve It?
Expert Opinions: important archeological site; New Seven Wonders
Fact: endangered by erosion
Reason: Need to preserve for further study

Claudia Zhang
Ms. Margolis, English
March 15

Machu Picchu: Still a Mystery

In the summer of 1911, American archaeologist Hiram Bingham and his team were searching for a city known only through legends. In Peru and other areas of South America, people told stories about "The Lost City of the Incas" that was supposedly built many centuries before. Bingham's group walked on foot and traveled on mules to journey from Cuzco to the Urubamba Valley in the Peruvian Andes. Bingham later reported that at times he feared for his life during the dangerous journey through the rugged mountains. Eventually, a farmer told them of ruins located at the top of a mountain. On July 24, led by a small group of peasants and an 11-year-old boy, Bingham first saw the site that natives called "old hill" or Machu Picchu (Cartwright).

This anecdote helps draw the reader into the essay.

Today, Machu Picchu has been visited by thousands of people. Terraces, walls, and stairways peek out from the sloping mountains, creating a stunning picture of ancient beauty. It has also been studied by some of the greatest archaeologists from around the world. But even though it is now one of the best known ancient sites, many mysteries remain ("Machu Picchu").

This recent photo shows the beauty of Machu Picchu.

Why Was It Built?

One of the mysteries surrounding Machu Picchu is its original purpose. Because it is so remote and shows such careful planning, it is clear that the city was carefully and intentionally built. Some archaeologists believe that the city was a royal estate for Inca nobles and emperors. Other guesses have included a women's retreat, a city created solely for the coronation of kings, a prison, or a site for testing new crops. Some point to the strong city walls as a reason to believe it served as a military fortress (Cartwright). The belief that Machu Picchu served as a religious site is supported by its geographic location, close to the mountains and other natural features that were important to the Inca (Reynolds). Historians are still searching for evidence to prove why such a beautiful and formidable city was built in the 15th century.

Why Was It Abandoned?

Evidence suggests that Machu Picchu was abandoned only about 100 years after it was built. Historians are not sure of the exact reason why. The Spanish had arrived in South America around this time, so some consider this a possible explanation for its abandonment. However, there is no evidence that the Spanish ever entered Machu Picchu. Some historians believe a smallpox epidemic forced the Inca to leave Machu Picchu. The people had no resistance to that disease and it traveled with people moving from place to place ahead of the Spanish forces. An Incan visitor

This paragraph introduces the central idea.

This photograph helps the reader understand the geography of the site.

This paragraph gives examples of reasons that people might have left Machu Picchu.

to Machu Picchu could have brought the dreadful disease (Burke). There was also a great drought in the area around the time, so some people believe the lack of water prompted people to leave the city behind (Cartwright).

Who Discovered It?

After visiting Machu Picchu in 1911, Bingham excavated artifacts from the site and brought them to Yale University. He also wrote several books about the area that prompted eager tourists to travel to Peru and make the same journey along the Inca Trail. Bingham's work was one of the reasons that Machu Picchu became a travel destination for people around the world ("Hiram Bingham").

Bingham became famous as the person that "discovered" Machu Picchu, but it was always well-known to local people. Other evidence indicates that there had been a visit to Machu Picchu by a German explorer about fifty years before Bingham ("Machu Picchu"). Many experts agree with the head of the Archeology Department at Peru's leading university, Dr. Julian Flores, who has stated, "Missionaries and other explorers arrived at Machu Picchu years before Bingham, beginning in the 19th century" (Burke 187).

Why Preserve It?

Modern Machu Picchu still has terraced fields and a complex irrigation system that served the different sectors of the city when the Inca people lived there ("Machu Picchu"). Dr. Flores states that "Machu Picchu may be the most important archeological site in the Americas" (Burke 188). In 2007, experts named Machu Picchu one of the New Seven Wonders of the World. Today, it is Peru's most visited site, but erosion caused by improper use could endanger one of the most beautiful and ancient sites in the world ("UNESCO"). The chart shows how the yearly influx of approximately 800,000 tourists leads to damage in the area.

You make good use of headings to organize the information. The question format ties into the idea that there are still puzzles to solve about Machu Picchu.

Your text explains that the commonly-accepted belief that Bingham "discovered" Machu Picchu is not true.

This quote from an expert helps clarify why it is important to preserve Machu Picchu.

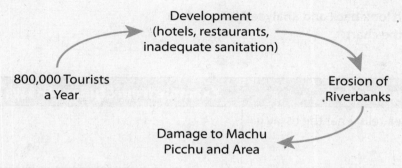

800,000 Tourists a Year → Development (hotels, restaurants, inadequate sanitation) → Erosion of Riverbanks → Damage to Machu Picchu and Area

This simple chart helps readers understand how tourism can lead to problems.

The government has taken steps to ensure that tourists exercise proper care when visiting the site. People around the world realize that it's important to protect the ruins in order to continue enjoying and studying its mysteries.

Works Cited

Burke, Winston. *The History of Peru.* New York: Oak Tree Publishing, 2010. Print.

Cartwright, Mark. "Machu Picchu," *Ancient History Encyclopedia,* 4 Mar. 2014. Web. 6 Mar. 2015.

"Hiram Bingham." *Encyclopædia Britannica. Encyclopædia Britannica Online.* Encyclopædia Britannica Inc., 2015. Web. 8 Mar. 2015.

"Machu Picchu." *Encyclopædia Britannica. Encyclopædia Britannica Online.* Encyclopædia Britannica Inc., 2015. Web. 6 Mar. 2015.

Reynolds, Helen. "The Wonders of the World." *World Archaeology,* 11 Dec. 2009: 69–75. Print.

"UNESCO Calls for Better Protection of Machu Picchu and Nearby Town." *IE Travel Blog.* International Expeditions, 15 June 2012. Web. 9 Mar. 2015.

Discuss and Decide

Why is Machu Picchu known as the "Lost City of the Incas"?

Terminology of Informative Essays

Read each term and explanation. Then look back and analyze each student model. Find an example to complete the chart.

Term	Explanation	Example from Student Essays
central idea	The **central idea** tells what the essay is mostly about.	
sub-topic	A **sub-topic** is one of several aspects (parts) of the central idea. The sub-topics explain the central idea.	
supporting details	**Supporting details** include anecdotes, commonly accepted beliefs, examples, expert opinions, and facts that explain each sub-topic.	
text structure	The **text structure** is the organizational pattern of an essay.	
domain-specific vocabulary	**Domain-specific vocabulary** is precise, content-specific words.	
text features	**Text features** are design elements that help organize the text, such as headings, boldface type, italic type, bulleted or numbered lists, sidebars, and graphic aids such as charts, maps, illustrations, or photographs.	

Prose Constructed-Reponse How do the text features support the reader in learning about the topic of the essay? Support your claim by citing text evidence.

_____

_____

_____

What can you teach about the Mayan and Egyptian pyramids?

You will read:

▶ **A MAGAZINE ARTICLE**
The Pyramids of Giza

▶ **DATA ANALYSIS**
The Great Pyramid at Giza

▶ **A TRAVEL GUIDE**
Visiting the Mayan Pyramids

▶ **AN INFOGRAPHIC**
El Castillo Mayan Pyramid
The Great Pyramid at Giza

You will write:

▶ **AN INFORMATIVE ESSAY**
Write an informative essay about the Mayan and Egyptian pyramids.

Source Materials for Step 2

AS YOU READ You will be writing an informative essay about the Mayan and Egyptian pyramids. Carefully study the sources in Step 2. For each text, annotate by underlining and circling information that may be useful to you when you write your essay.

Source 1: Magazine Article

THE PYRAMIDS OF GIZA

by Helena Gustafson

When you hear the word *pyramids,* what picture do you see in your head? More likely than not, you see three magnificent stone structures rising out of the desert sands. These are the pyramids of Giza, Egypt, famous not only for their stupendous size and dramatic shape, but also for the astonishing skill with which they were built thousands of years ago.

The pyramids at Giza

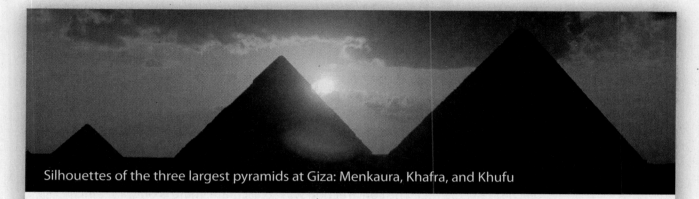

Silhouettes of the three largest pyramids at Giza: Menkaura, Khafra, and Khufu

The three pyramids at Giza were designed as monumental tombs for pharaohs (kings) of Egypt, to house their bodies after death and to help them achieve eternal life in the afterworld. Each was made by and for a different pharaoh: King Khufu built the Great Pyramid (the biggest) first, around 2550 BC; King Khafra built the second pyramid around 2520 BC; King Menkaura built the third (smallest of the three and last) in about 2490 BC.

Although there are a few passageways and chambers inside each pyramid, the structures are mostly solid stone. They were designed to be permanently sealed after the bodies of the pharaohs were placed inside. Neither the inside nor the outside of the pyramid had any public function other than to memorialize the powerful king buried inside.

As impressive as they look today, the Giza pyramids were even more striking when first built. Originally, the four faces of each pyramid were covered with a smooth layer of bright white limestone blocks that would have gleamed and glittered in the sunlight. After these casing blocks fell or were stripped off hundreds of years ago, many were hauled away and used to build mosques and houses in the city of Cairo nearby.

The pyramids at Giza have been astonishing humanity for more than 4,500 years. Successive generations of travelers, invaders, and explorers have come across them and marveled: Ancient Greeks, Arab conquerors, even Napoleon.

Even in Ancient Egyptian times, the Giza pyramids were antiques. They were more than a thousand years old at the time of King Tutankhamen. The largest pyramid at Giza is the only one of the Seven Wonders of the Ancient World that remains; to this day, it is a sight that amazes all who see it.

From *History Wonders*, May 2016, pages 7–8.

Discuss and Decide

If you were to write a travel brochure advertising a visit to the Giza pyramids, which facts would you highlight and why?

Source 2: Data Analysis

The Great Pyramid at Giza	
Pyramid Statistics	
Height	Originally 481 feet high, the pyramid currently stands at 450 feet. It is higher than the Statue of Liberty, St. Peter's Basilica in Rome, or Big Ben in London.
Base	Each side is 756 feet. The construction was so accurate, there is only a 7.9-inch difference between the longest and shortest sides of the base. Almost ten football fields would fit into the base.
Accuracy	The blocks were shaped and placed so perfectly that even today it is not possible to squeeze a knife blade between them.
How Was the Great Pyramid at Giza Built?	
Skilled laborers	Some archaeologists estimate it took 4,000 skilled laborers at least 20 years.
Materials	The pyramid is comprised of approximately 2,300,000 limestone and granite blocks, each weighing an average of 2.5 tons, for a total weight of 5,750,000 tons.
Transport	Some of the stone blocks were transported by boat from quarries as far as 500 miles away.
Construction	Stones were hauled into place on sleds pulled by teams of at least 30 men, without the help of engines, pulleys, or even wheeled carts.
Simple tools	The builders had copper, bronze, wood, and stone tools—no iron or steel. The Great Pyramid was built using simple, hand-held tools such as chisels, mallets, rock pounders and polishers, and small wooden clamps.
Largest pieces of stone	The largest slabs of stone are above the King's Chamber, inside the Great Pyramid. They weigh about 50 tons each.
Ramp	Archaeologists suggest that a huge ramp was built, allowing stones to be hauled to the top. The ramp would have had to be raised as the pyramid grew taller.
Notable Records	
Tallest man-made structure	The Great Pyramid was the tallest man-made structure for more than 3,800 years.
Visibility	The three pyramids at Giza are visible from space.
Alignment	The four sides of the Great Pyramid align almost exactly with true north, south, east, and west; without the magnetic compass, the builders probably used the stars to make their calculations.

Source: *What's So Great About the Great Pyramid of Giza?* by Jamal Higgins
(Minneapolis: Midwest Press, 2012), page 105.

Source 3: Travel Guide

✈ **Visiting the**

MaYaN PYRaMiDS

Where can I find the Mayan pyramids?

If you want to find a Mayan pyramid, go to Central America! The Maya were a Mesoamerican civilization that arose around 1500 BC. They built most of their pyramids between the 3rd and 9th century AD, all across eastern Mexico, Belize, Guatemala, Honduras, and El Salvador.

What do they look like?

While Mayan pyramids come in a variety of shapes and sizes, most are step pyramids;

The ruins at Chichen Itza, a city in the Yucatán built by the Mayans. A Chac Mool statue reclines in the foreground. At the spring and autumn equinoxes, the shadow cast by the pyramid's steps looks like a snake crawling up its side.

The entrance to the pyramid is at the very top, not the bottom.

the sides are not smooth but instead rise up in stages, like giant stairs. Often there are one or more actual staircases built on top of the steps, leading to a temple or sanctuary at the top.

Compared to the Egyptian pyramids at Giza, Mayan pyramids are mostly smaller, but steeper and more ornate. They were built of stone blocks held together with lime mortar. Some were covered with plaster and painted. The Maya were expert astronomers, so their pyramids were positioned and constructed to note important points in the calendar, such as the solstice and equinox.

The pyramids played an important part in the religious and community life of the people.

Mayan pyramids functioned as temples, whether or not they were also tombs of high-

Looking up the terraces toward the top of the pyramid.

ranking officials. Only priests were allowed to climb the stairs to the top. There they performed religious rituals, including human sacrifices of war prisoners, whose blood was offered as food for the gods. The pyramids were often part of large complexes that included palaces, ball courts, plazas, and courtyards.

Sometimes a new pyramid was built on top of an old one. If you were to dig down inside a Mayan pyramid built in, say, AD 800, you might find the ruins of one built hundreds of years earlier.

What else do I need to know for my visit?

Mayan civilization flourished between around AD 250 and 900, at which point it went into a sudden and mysterious decline. Many cities and towns were abandoned and completely swallowed up by the jungle. Although the local people may have known about them—and although Spanish conquistadors had written about them—many of the most impressive Mayan archeological sites were not "rediscovered" by Europeans until 1839 and later. Even now there are Mayan pyramids hiding in the thick jungle, waiting to be "discovered" by an intrepid explorer.

Maybe that explorer will be you!

The Mayan Civilization

From *Trekking Through Central America* by Forrest Anderson, 2nd edition (New York: Books for Travelers, 2014), pages 47–50.

Discuss and Decide

Explain at least three differences between Mayan and Egyptian pyramids, and the reason for one of these differences. Cite text evidence in your discussion.

1. Analyze   2. Practice   3. Perform

Source 4: Infographic

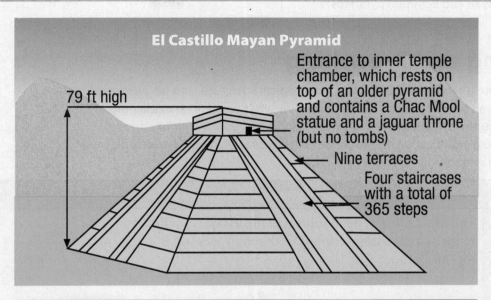

El Castillo Mayan Pyramid

79 ft high

Entrance to inner temple chamber, which rests on top of an older pyramid and contains a Chac Mool statue and a jaguar throne (but no tombs)

Nine terraces

Four staircases with a total of 365 steps

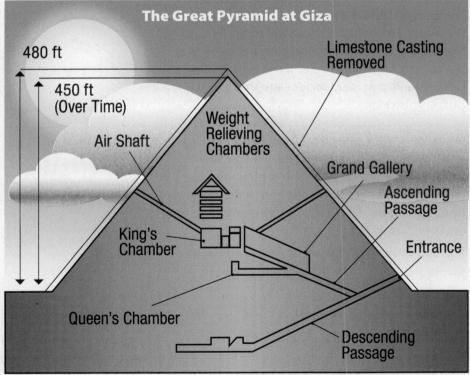

The Great Pyramid at Giza

480 ft

450 ft (Over Time)

Limestone Casting Removed

Air Shaft

Weight Relieving Chambers

Grand Gallery

Ascending Passage

King's Chamber

Entrance

Queen's Chamber

Descending Passage

Source: *The World's Great Pyramids,* website created by Darlene Tanaka, accessed 20 April 2015.

Discuss and Decide

What information about Egyptian pyramids does the infographic provide that the previous two sources do not?

Planning and Prewriting

When you write an informative essay using a topical structure, you begin by writing a central idea, a specific statement that identifies what you will be explaining in your essay. You then decide which sub-topics (or parts) you will write about to convey the most significant aspects of the central idea. Each of the sub-topics will be elaborated with details to fully explain it.

Planning Your Essay		
Topic	The **topic** is the general subject of the essay. In the sample essays in this unit, the topic was Machu Picchu.	Topic:
Central Idea	The **central idea** is a sentence that asserts the writer's main point about the topic. For example, in the student model on pages 46–49, the topic is Machu Picchu and the central idea is "Machu Picchu is an ancient site that still puzzles historians."	Your central idea:
Sub-topics	In planning your essay, you need to identify the **sub-topics** of your central idea. All sub-topics should explain or describe the central idea. Each sub-topic should be distinct, or different from the others. If two sub-topics overlap or are very closely related, combine them. The sub-topics in the student model on pages 46–49 are • Why Was It Built? • Why Was It Abandoned? • Who Discovered It? • Why Preserve It?	Your sub-topics: 1) 2) 3) 4) Depending on your central idea, you may not have four sub-topics. You may have only two or three.
Details	Each sub-topic is supported with **details** from the source(s). You will plan out the details to include on the next planning page.	See the next planning page.

1. Analyze   2. Practice   3. Perform

Finalize Your Plan

Use your responses and notes from the previous pages to create a detailed plan for your essay. Fill in the chart below.

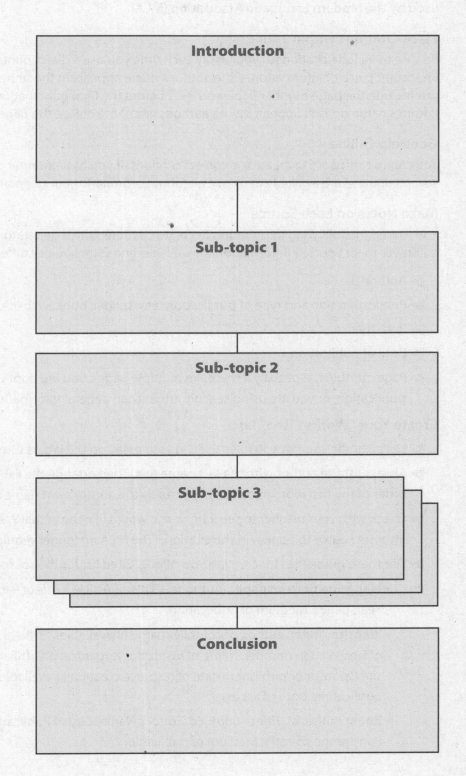

► Hook your audience with an interesting detail, question, or quotation.

► Clearly state your central idea.

► Develop each sub-topic with supporting details. Each sub-topic needs at least two supporting details. These details may include:
- anecdotes
- commonly accepted beliefs
- examples
- expert opinions
- facts

Reminder! Use your chosen text structure to develop your topic. The number of boxes in the graphic may change to work with your plan. Just make a revised copy of the graphic on another sheet of paper.

► Summarize the information about your sub-topics and restate your central idea.

► Include an insight that follows from and supports your central idea.

Within the graphic:

Introduction

Sub-topic 1

Sub-topic 2

Sub-topic 3

Conclusion

Cite Your Sources

A credible informative essay is based on reliable sources that are cited within the essay and listed at the end. Many teachers and organizations support the format used by the Modern Language Association (MLA).

Place Citations within Your Essay

Be sure to include citations in your essay each time you use a direct quote or an important piece of information. If the author's name appears in the same sentence, just include the page number in parentheses before the final punctuation. If the author's name doesn't appear, list the author's last name before the page number.

Get Help Online

You can use software to create the correct citations. If you have Internet access, several of these are available at http://mlaformat.org/mla-format-generator/.

Make Notes on Each Source

You'll need the following information to create citations with a generator or to complete them yourself (information for websites and print sources differ slightly):

▶ Author(s)

▶ Publication title and type of publication: newspaper, book, website, etc.

▶ Publisher

▶ Date of publication

▶ Page numbers, especially if there are multiple pages, you are quoting directly from the publication, or you are using specific rather than general information

Create Your "Works Cited" List

▶ List all of the sources you have used in your essay on the Works Cited list at the end.

▶ Always list the author with the last name first. Then arrange the list by alphabetical order of the first word in each entry (usually the author's last name).

▶ Check with your teacher to see if he or she would like the actual Web address (URL) for an Internet source to appear in the citation. (The MLA no longer requires it.)

▶ Use these guidelines for creating your Works Cited list for the sources on pages 52–57:

- **Magazine or Newspaper:** Author(s). "Title of Article." *Title of Periodical* Day Month Year: pages. Medium of publication.

- **Website:** Editor, author, or compiler name (if available). "Title of Page." *Name of Site.* Version number. Name of institution/organization affiliated with the site (sponsor or publisher), date of resource creation (if available). Medium of publication. Date of access.

- **Book:** Author(s). *Title of Book.* Ed. Editor's Name. City of Publication: Publisher, Year. Page range of entry. Medium of publication.

Draft Your Essay

▶ **Audience:** Your teacher, your classmates, and possibly others with whom you might want to share your essay

▶ **Purpose:** Demonstrate your understanding of the specific requirements of an informative essay with a comparison/contrast text structure.

▶ **Style:** Use a formal and objective tone.

▶ **Transitions:** Use words and phrases such as *furthermore, consequently, as an illustration,* or *similarly* to create cohesion, or flow.

Revise

Add Transitions

As you reread your draft, ask yourself whether all the connections between ideas are clear. Add transitions to help readers understand the relationships between your central idea, sub-topics, and supporting details.

Review the following list of transitions that can help you connect your ideas. Transitions can be used at the beginning of a paragraph to show how it relates to the previous one. They are also useful for linking the ideas and details within each paragraph.

▶ **Add an idea or detail:** in addition, also, furthermore, as well as, too

▶ **Compare:** similar(ly), in the same way, also

▶ **Contrast:** on the other hand, by contrast, different, however, but

▶ **Emphasize:** more/most important(ly), key, it's crucial to note that

▶ **Generalize:** in general, in most cases, most of the time, on the whole

▶ **Give an example:** as an illustration, for example, for instance

▶ **Restate:** in other words, or, another way to look at it is

▶ **Point out an exception:** however, on the other hand, an exception is

▶ **Sequence:** first, second, third, then, next, finally, last, at the same time, a long time ago, immediately before/after

▶ **Show cause and effect:** because, as a result, consequently, due to

▶ **Summarize:** in summary, to summarize, the short answer is

Add Text Features

Another step in your revision process is to assess your use of text features. Have you used enough of them to make the organization of your essay clear? Could you add more to improve the structure or to illustrate key ideas?

Review the student models on pages 42–49 to see how each writer used a title, sub-topic headings, graphics, and captions. Then follow these steps:

▶ **Think about your title.** The title of your essay should indicate its topic, but it doesn't have to be boring. Craft a title that will make your readers want to know more. For example, an essay about the city of Paris could be titled "Paris: City of Lights," "The Romance of Paris," or "Paris Is More Than Just the Eiffel Tower."

▶ **Check your sub-topic headings.** Including a heading for each of your sub-topics is a great way to make your organization clear to readers. Make sure that the text following each heading is all about that sub-topic. Then consider the phrasing of your headings. You might want to state each sub-topic directly in a word or brief phrase. Or, you might want to take a more literary approach and pick out a colorful phrase from the text to use for the heading. This phrase might be one that you wrote or one you've quoted from a source.

▶ **Define domain-specific vocabulary.** Have you used any specialized terms that might not be familiar to your readers? For example, an essay about Egyptian art might use words such as *amulet* and *hieroglyphs*. Skim your essay for any such words and add definitions. You might also use *italic* or **boldface** type for the first appearance of each domain-specific term.

▶ **Include appropriate graphics.** You've no doubt heard that "a picture is worth a thousand words." Are there any photographs, drawings, charts, diagrams, or maps that would help readers better understand your topic? If so, can you create these graphics, or does it make sense to find something online? If you are using a computer, you might download images from the Internet (being sure to cite the sources) or scan something that you create on paper.

Revision Checklist: Self Evaluation

 If you drafted your essay on the computer, you may wish to print it out so that you can more easily evaluate it.

Use the checklist below to guide your analysis.

Ask Yourself	Tips	Revision Strategies
1. Does the introduction grab the audience's attention?	Underline sentences in the introduction that engage readers.	Add an interesting question, fact, or observation to get the reader's attention.
2. Is each sub-topic supported by textual evidence, facts, and concrete details?	Circle supporting evidence.	Add supporting evidence if necessary.
3. Are appropriate and varied transitions used to connect ideas?	Place a checkmark next to each transitional word or phrase.	Add transitional words or phrases where needed to clarify the relationships between ideas.
4. Does the concluding section sum up key ideas? Does it give the audience something to think about?	Double underline the summary of key points in the concluding section. Underline the insight offered to readers.	Add an overarching view of key points or a final observation about the significance of the comparison and contrast.
5. Do text features make the organization clear and illustrate key ideas?	Circle text features, including the title, sub-topic headings, definitions of domain-specific vocabulary, and graphics.	Add text features as needed to clarify the structure, define specialized terms, and illustrate important ideas.
6. Are sources cited both within the text and in a Works Cited list?	Highlight specific facts, details, and quotations that come from external sources.	Add citations within the text as needed. Revise any entries in the Works Cited list that are not correctly formatted.

Revision Checklist: Peer Review

Exchange your essay with a classmate, or read it aloud to your partner. As you read and comment on your classmate's essay, focus on how thoroughly the central idea and sub-topics have been developed with supporting details. Help each other identify parts of the drafts that need strengthening, reworking, or even a new approach.

What To Look For	Notes for My Partner
1. Does the introduction grab the audience's attention?	
2. Is each sub-topic supported by textual evidence, facts, and concrete details?	
3. Are appropriate and varied transitions used to connect ideas?	
4. Does the concluding section sum up the central idea? Does it give the audience something to think about?	
5. Do text features make the organization clear and illustrate key ideas?	
6. Are sources cited both within the text and in a Works Cited list?	

Edit

 Edit your essay to correct spelling, grammar, and punctuation errors.

PERFORM THE TASK

In what ways were the Maya, the Aztecs, and the Inca advanced for their time?

You will read:

▶ **THREE INFORMATIVE ARTICLES**

Mayan Civilization

Aztecs

The Inca

You will write:

▶ **AN INFORMATIVE ESSAY**
In what ways were the Maya, the Aztecs, and the Inca advanced for their time?

Mayan Civilization

by Suzanne Hopkins

AS YOU READ *Identify key terms that you might want to use in your essay.*

NOTES

Long before the rise of the Inca and Aztec Empires, Mayan civilization flourished in Central America. The Maya first settled in the region as early as 1500 BC, growing maize and living in small agricultural communities. But by about AD 200, these villages were becoming cities. At its height, Mayan civilization included more than 40 cities, each with a population of 5,000 to 50,000 people. The cities had huge stone buildings, including palaces, pyramids, and temples. Each city-state was ruled by a king.

Mayan Society

Mayan society was hierarchical, divided by both class and
10   profession. Below the king was a class of nobles; a middle class was composed of priests and commoners; at the lowest level were slaves.

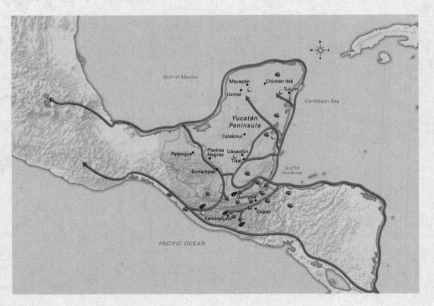

1. Analyze   2. Practice   3. Perform

The Maya were never an empire. Although the cities shared the same culture, each operated independently. They traded goods with each other, including salt, shells, cotton, corn, rubber, incense, feathers, jade, flint, obsidian, and granite that were carried in huge dugout canoes along rivers and around coasts. They also fought wars, but these were on a small scale, one city against another.

A Time of Prosperity

For many centuries, the Maya prospered. They studied the stars and developed sophisticated and accurate calendars; practiced elaborate (if
20 gory) religious rituals and worshiped a crowded pantheon of gods and goddesses; they developed complex hieroglyphic writing that they used to record historical and religious events; they had a mathematical system based on the unit 20. Their craftsmen and artists produced fine goods made of cotton, feathers, clay, wood, and precious metals and
30 stones, among other materials.

Decline

Yet by AD 800, Mayan civilization was in decline. While the reasons are not fully understood, archaeologists believe that the cities had grown so large, there were not enough farmers left to supply them with food. In addition, the farmland was becoming overused, the soil depleted. Food production
40 plummeted, and famine forced people to leave the urban centers.

THE MAYAN CIVILIZATION

1500 BC
Earliest evidence of Mayan civilization

AD 200
Mayan villages grow into cities lasting hundreds of years

800
Mayan civilization in decline for unknown reasons

950
Mayan cities empty and abandoned

1500s
Spanish conquer all of former empire

By AD 950, the great Mayan cities were mostly abandoned, the population dispersed into small agricultural villages. The jungle swallowed up the empty cities. The Mayan people, however, were still around when the Spanish conquistadors arrived. And they are still around today.

Though the Spanish conquered the Maya in the mid-1500s and founded cities on Mayan lands, temples and monuments remain as a testimony to the Mayans' achievements. These structures attract
50 tourists from around the world, ensuring that the Maya will never be forgotten.

From *Great Civilizations* website. Historical Media Group, undated. Retrieved September 12, 2014.

Close Read

1. Explain ways in which the Maya were advanced for their time, citing text evidence.

_____

_____

_____

2. Explain possible reasons for the decline of the Mayan empire. Cite text evidence in your response.

_____

_____

_____

Source 2: Informative Article

AZTECS

by Jose Maldonado from *Travel in Mexico*, March 2012, p. 62

Long ago, around AD 1345, a group of people in central Mexico wandered in search of a new home. These people were the Aztecs, and Aztec legend says that a prophecy led them to a group of islands on Lake Texcoco, in the Valley of Mexico. Their settlement would eventually become the great city Tenochtitlán.

As the last to arrive, the Aztec were at first ruled over by more powerful city-states in the area. But, after making alliances with some of these city-states, the Aztecs were able to defeat their overlords in 1428. Soon they began conquering other tribes across Mexico, and

10 Tenochtitlán became the center of a powerful Aztec empire.

AS YOU READ *Identify details that support the main idea.*

NOTES

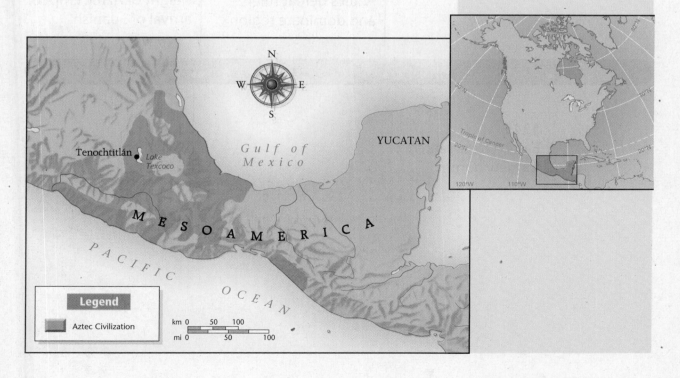

The Great City

At its height in 1519, the city covered about five square miles and had between 250 and 400 thousand inhabitants. It had temples, palaces, a great market, houses, and gardens. Although the city was built on a swamp, the Aztecs were able to adapt. They traveled around and through Tenochtitlán by canoe. Several raised causeways connected the island city to the mainland. They farmed special plots of land called chinampas (also known as "floating gardens")—raised areas of land built in the lake, separated by canals, where they grew maize and other crops.

20   Building cities was not the Aztecs' only accomplishment. They used picture writing to record political and religious history; they used calendars and had a mathematical system based on the number 20. They wove cotton cloth, made pottery, carved in stone and other materials, made musical instruments and elaborate costumes of feathers.

THE AZTEC CIVILIZATION

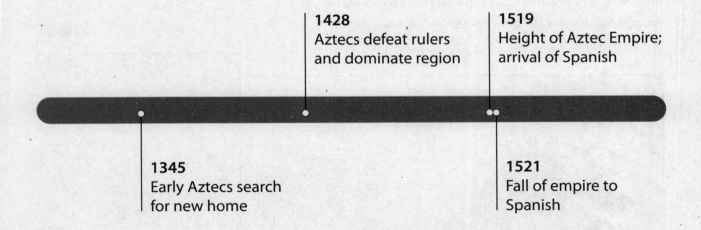

1428
Aztecs defeat rulers
and dominate region

1519
Height of Aztec Empire;
arrival of Spanish

1345
Early Aztecs search
for new home

1521
Fall of empire to
Spanish

A Hierarchical Society

Aztec society was strictly hierarchical, ruled over by a godlike emperor. Religion was an important part of everyday life, and a gory one, as they believed that human sacrifice was needed to keep the sun alive. The Aztec were harsh rulers; they demanded high tributes and 30 were constantly fighting in order to keep up a steady supply of captives to use as human sacrifice. The harsh way they ruled their empire helped to undermine them in the end.

Decline

In 1519, Hernán Cortés and his army arrived in Tenochtitlán. When the Spanish first saw the city, they thought they must be dreaming. It was larger and more impressive than any Spanish city of the time. Vastly outnumbered, the Spanish conquistador took the Aztec emperor Montezuma II hostage and began a siege in Tenochtitlán that the Aztec could not withstand. Within three years, and with the help of the local tribes who were eager to break away from Aztec rule, Cortés was able to 40 crush the Aztecs and bring about the complete collapse of their empire. The last Aztec emperor surrendered the city to Cortés in 1521, thus ending one of the most famous empires in history.

Close Read

1. In what ways were the Aztecs advanced for their time? Cite text evidence in your response.

_____

_____

_____

2. Cite two reasons from the text showing how the Aztecs' harsh rule contributed to the fall of their society.

_____

_____

_____

Source 3: Informative Article

THE INCA

by Akbar Patel

Understanding South America website, New Front Publishing, Inc., 2008

AS YOU READ *Identify topics addressed in this article that have also been addressed in the previous two.*

NOTES

Sometime in the twelfth century BC, the first Inca ruler is said to have moved his tribe to what is now Cuzco, high in the Andes. Until the fourteenth century, the Inca lived there peacefully with their neighbors. But then they began a campaign of territorial expansion that would eventually make Cuzco the capital of a vast empire.

Establishing an Empire

Successive generations of Incan rulers worked to expand Incan territory through war and conquest. At its height, the Inca Empire stretched more than 2,000 miles along the west coast of South America and governed millions of people. The farthest reaches of the empire

10 were connected with well-constructed roads and strong rope bridges. An elaborate system of relay runners enabled messages to be carried 250 miles a day; runners made the 1,250-mile journey from Quito (a city in the far north) to Cuzco in just five days.

THE INCA CIVILIZATION

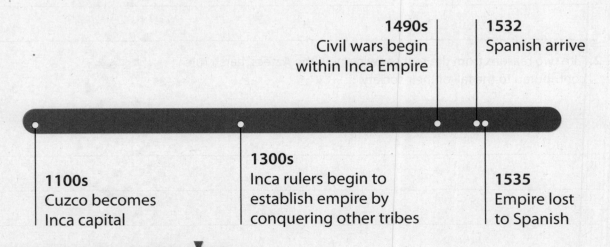

1100s
Cuzco becomes
Inca capital

1300s
Inca rulers begin to
establish empire by
conquering other tribes

1490s
Civil wars begin
within Inca Empire

1532
Spanish arrive

1535
Empire lost
to Spanish

1. Analyze   2. Practice   3. Perform

Incan society was hierarchical and highly centralized, with the god-like emperor at the top of the social pyramid, followed by provincial governors, local rulers and leaders, and finally the common people. The common people paid taxes and tributes and worked for the central government. The Inca did not have a writing system, but they were able to keep track of trade goods and stockpiles with a special system of
20 knotted strings called a quipu. Religion was an important part of life.

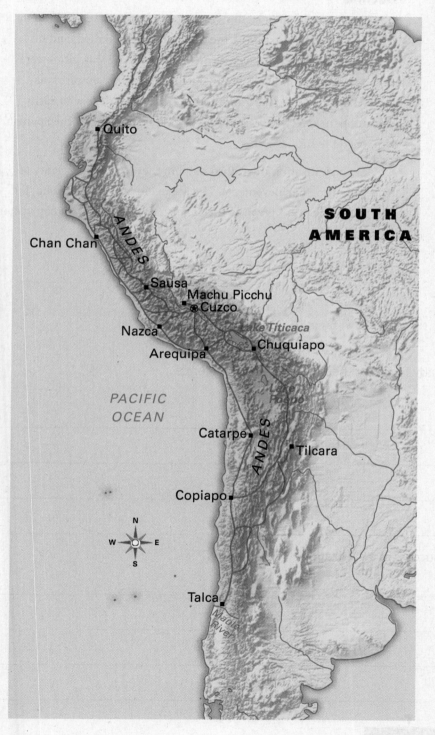

Economy

The Inca were farmers, growing potatoes as well as other crops, often in terraces cut into the high mountainsides. They had llamas to carry loads, for wool, and for meat. They were also skilled craftsmen, building impressive cities of stone, weaving exquisite woolen cloth, and making pottery, jewelry, and many other useful and ornamental objects.

Decline

The Spanish conquistador Francisco Pizarro arrived in Peru in 1531—a very bad time for the Inca. An emperor had died, and his two sons fought over the succession. In the ensuing war, cities were devastated, the economy was damaged, and the Inca empire was
30 divided. Pizarro used his guns, horses, and some trickery to easily defeat the Inca. New diseases brought to the Americas by the Spanish weakened the Inca as well.

Incan civilization was wiped out, but they left behind plenty of evidence of their achievements. The Incan city of Machu Picchu, for example, was never known to the Spanish invaders, but you can visit it today.

Close Read

1. In what ways were the Inca advanced for their time? Cite text evidence in your response.

_____

_____

_____

_____

2. Cite evidence of the Inca's success as a civilization.

_____

_____

_____

_____

Part 2: Write

Plan

Use the graphic organizer to help you outline the structure of your informative essay.

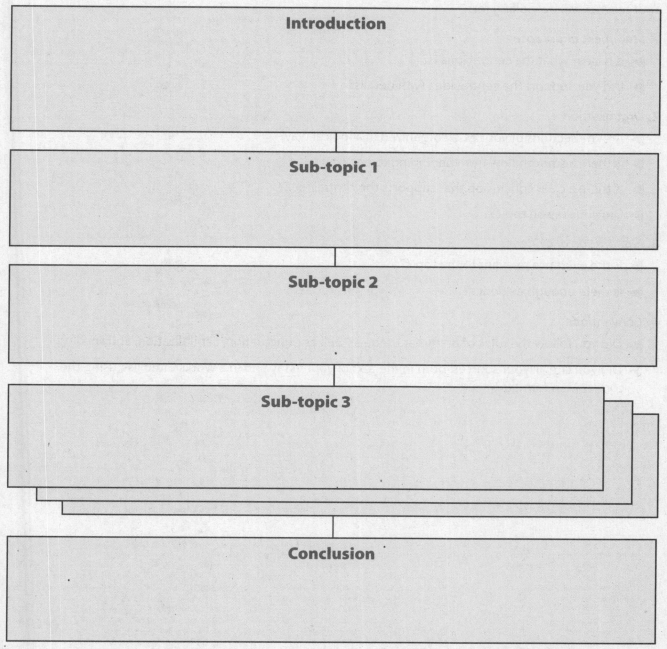

Introduction

Sub-topic 1

Sub-topic 2

Sub-topic 3

Conclusion

Draft

 Use your notes and completed graphic organizer to write a first draft of your essay.

Revise and Edit

 Look back over your essay and compare it to the Evaluation Criteria. Revise your essay and edit it to correct spelling, grammar, and punctuation errors.

Evaluation Criteria

Your teacher will be looking for:

1. Statement of purpose
- ▶ Is it clear what the central idea is?
- ▶ Did you support the central idea with details?

2. Organization
- ▶ Are the sections of your essay organized in a logical way?
- ▶ Is there a smooth flow from beginning to end?
- ▶ Is there a clear conclusion that supports the central idea?
- ▶ Did you stay on topic?

3. Elaboration of evidence
- ▶ Is the evidence relevant to the topic?
- ▶ Is there enough evidence?

4. Conventions
- ▶ Did you follow the rules of grammar usage as well as punctuation, capitalization, and spelling?
- ▶ Did you cite all your sources, both in the text of your essay and in a Works Cited list, using the correct MLA formats?

Techniques

Literary Analysis

© Houghton Mifflin Harcourt Publishing Company

STEP 1

ANALYZE THE MODEL

Evaluate an analysis of E. E. Cummings's poem "Spring is like a perhaps hand."

STEP 2

PRACTICE THE TASK

Write an analysis of how Shakespeare uses irony in Mark Antony's speech.

STEP 3

PERFORM THE TASK

Write a literary analysis of how W. F. Harvey plays with story structure and timing to create horror.

Unlike nonfiction texts, literary texts—poems, stories, dramas—are not written solely to give information. They are written primarily to have an effect on the reader.

At its best, literature can cause you to react on many levels. You can be gripped by a story line or charmed by a character. The words might create a beautiful image in your mind. The mood may capture your imagination and even alter your own mood as you read.

Writers help readers see even the most familiar things in a new way. They use literary techniques to draw their readers into unique experiences, which may be delightful or terrifying, unsettling or comforting. The way a horror story is told, for example, creates the twists and surprises we have come to expect and love in that genre of literature.

IN THIS UNIT, you will analyze responses by two students to a free verse poem by E. E. Cummings. Then, you will write an analysis of the use of irony in Mark Antony's famous speech in Shakespeare's *Julius Caesar*. Finally, you will write an analysis of how W. F. Harvey plays with text structure to create a chilling impact on the reader in his short story "August Heat."

ANALYZE THE MODEL

What techniques can a poet use to describe the coming of spring?

You will read:

▶ **AN INFORMATIVE ARTICLE**
The Modernist Poetry of E. E. Cummings

▶ **A POEM**
"Spring is like a perhaps hand"

You will analyze:

▶ **TWO STUDENT MODELS**
Winter Becomes Spring
The Gentle Hand of Spring

Source Materials for Step 1

Mr. Winter assigned his class a poem by E. E. Cummings to read and analyze. He also provided this article about the poet's techniques. The notes in the side column were written by Valerie Jones, a student in Mr. Winter's class.

The Modernist Poetry of E. E. Cummings

E. E. Cummings (1894–1962) was a rebel of the poetry world. His unique style breaks all the rules of grammar, punctuation, and poetic form. A champion of the individual, Cummings uses his poems to declare war on conformity, conventional ideas, and commercialism. Elements of his style include the following:

- **Free verse.** Cummings's poems do not have regular stanza structures or predictable patterns of rhyme.
- **Unconventional mechanics.** Cummings ignores the normal rules of capitalization and punctuation. He uses these mechanics to emphasize key ideas and to make readers stop and think about his subjects in a new light.
- **Invented compounds.** Words such as *mostpeople* and *squarerootofminusone* are examples of how Cummings mashes words together to create new compounds.
- **Changed parts of speech.** Cummings likes to use words in new ways, such as using *didn't* and *because* as nouns.
- **Syntax.** His grammatical wordplay includes rearranging the usual order of words. For example, one poem takes place in "a pretty how town," instead of "how pretty a town."
- **Enjambment.** Phrases and sentences often break across lines and stanzas in unexpected ways.

Despite the boldly original style of Cummings's poems, his themes are familiar. Like lyric poets throughout the ages, he celebrates the joy and wonder of life and the glory of the individual.

Source: *And Poetry 4 All* website, People's Poetry, Inc., January 2015.

> *I guess he didn't write sonnets or other forms that follow strict rules.*

> *His use of language sounds really interesting and playful.*

> *I wonder if his unusual techniques are effective in conveying these themes.*

Discuss and Decide

With a group, discuss the poetic techniques listed in the article. Which ones would make a poem challenging to read? Which would make a poem especially fun or interesting to read? Cite evidence for your ideas.

Spring is like a perhaps hand

by E. E. Cummings

"Perhaps" is not usually used as an adjective.

Spring is like a perhaps hand
(which comes carefully
out of Nowhere) arranging
a window, into which people look (while

5 people stare

Why no comma after "changing"?

arranging and changing placing
carefully there a strange
thing and a known thing here) and

changing everything carefully

This phrase stayed together in line 1, but here it breaks across lines.

10 spring is like a perhaps
Hand in a window
(carefully to
and fro moving New and
Old things, while

15 people stare carefully

Without punctuation, readers must figure out what is done "carefully."

moving a perhaps
fraction of flower here placing
an inch of air there) and

Why only 5 capital letters?

without breaking anything.

From *Complete Poems: 1904–1962* by E. E. Cummings (New York: Liveright Publishing Corporation, 2013), page 47.

Discuss and Decide

Review Valerie's notes in the side column. Then discuss your initial reactions to the poem with a partner. How are your reactions like or unlike Valerie's? Cite specific evidence from the text.

Analyze Two Student Models for Step 1

Read Valerie's literary analysis closely. The red side notes are the comments from her teacher, Mr. Winter.

Valerie Jones
Mr. Winter, English
March 24

Winter Becomes Spring

In the lyric poem "Spring is like a perhaps hand," E. E. Cummings uses a simile to compare spring to a hand rearranging items in a window display. His free verse poem creates an image of the gradual and uncertain morphing of winter into spring. He explores this familiar theme in his own unique style, with unusual word choices, unexpected line breaks, and odd capitalization and punctuation.

A common technique of Cummings's is changing a word from one part of speech to another ("The Modernist Poetry of E. E. Cummings"). In the first line of this poem, he uses *perhaps* (usually an adverb) as an adjective to describe the "hand" of springtime. I know that here, in the rural Northeast, it can be hard to know exactly when winter becomes spring. There might still be snow on the ground near where the first daffodils are emerging. Maybe spring has come, or maybe— perhaps—the wintery weather will continue. By using *perhaps* to describe spring, Cummings perfectly captures this idea.

Cummings makes good use of enjambment, breaking lines in unexpected but meaningful places. In line 15, "carefully" at first seems to describe the way that "people stare." A closer reading shows that it actually describes "moving" in the next line (16). This line break makes readers slow down and really think about what is happening. The spring "hand" is at work everywhere, even if people do not notice all the subtle changes. The way that "carefully" is tucked into a line where it almost doesn't belong mirrors the way springtime gradually, almost imperceptibly, changes the winter landscape.

It's interesting that Cummings capitalizes only five words—*Spring, Nowhere, Hand, New,* and *Old* (1, 3, 11, 13, 14). These are probably the most important words in the poem. Spring is the topic. Nowhere is the "place" from which spring arrives. This points to the mystery of nature and the seasons: Where does spring go during the rest of the year? Nowhere, and yet it is no longer here. The next capitalized word, *Hand,* creates the poem's key image of spring as a window dresser. *New* and *Old* stress the change from old winter to new spring.

> The capitals are odd, but your explanation is interesting and plausible.

Another hallmark of Cummings's poetry is his unusual use of punctuation ("The Modernist Poetry of E. E. Cummings"). In this poem, punctuation is sometimes missing where the reader would expect it. For example, in line 6, Cummings could have placed a comma between "arranging and changing" and "placing / carefully." By running these two phrases together, he again emphasizes that spring is busy all around us. One change spills into another, until everything is transformed.

> I like your analysis of that missing comma! At first it might seem confusing, but you've made a great guess about what ideas the poet wanted to convey.

Although Cummings's poem addresses a familiar topic, the arrival of spring, his use of unconventional techniques makes it fresh and new. Readers may struggle at first to untangle the unusual syntax and language use, but by the end of the poem the idea of the "perhaps hand" seems like the perfect metaphor for spring. Spring arrives so gently and so gradually that it accomplishes its task "without breaking anything" (19).

Works Cited

Cummings, E. E. "Spring is like a perhaps hand." *Complete Poems: 1904–1962*. New York: Liveright Publishing Corporation, 2013. 47. Print.

"The Modernist Poetry of E. E. Cummings." *And Poetry 4 All*. People's Poetry, Inc., Jan. 2015. Web. 20 Mar. 2015.

Discuss and Decide

With a group, decide whether or not you agree with Valerie's interpretation of the poem. Cite text evidence in your response.

In her essay, Valerie explored several of Cummings's techniques. Her classmate Atul took a different approach, exploring one technique used in several places. Read Atul's literary analysis and Mr. Winter's comments.

Atul Patel
Mr. Winter, English
March 24

The Gentle Hand of Spring

E. E. Cummings is a modern poet in many ways. Although he explores many of the same themes as traditional lyric poets, he ignores the usual rules of grammar, punctuation, and capitalization ("The Modernist Poetry of E. E. Cummings"). Even his use of enjambment, a tried-and-true technique of poets through the ages, has a fresh new twist. In his poem "Spring is like a perhaps hand," Cummings uses enjambment to support his description of spring as a gentle hand that changes everything around us in gradual, subtle ways that can be hard to perceive.

The first stanza provides several examples. In lines 2–4, two meaningful phrases are divided across lines: "(which comes carefully / out of Nowhere) arranging / a window. . . ." The way that the words "out of Nowhere)" break into line 3 creates a physical image on the page of how spring appears suddenly and unexpectedly. The line break after "arranging" emphasizes the idea of placing things carefully. Just as the poet has chosen to place "a window" on the next line, the hand of spring places its seasonal changes in carefully chosen locations. Anyone who has ever been surprised to see a crocus popping up in a spot that was just bare dirt yesterday can understand this idea about spring's wonders.

Line 9 of the poem is a stanza all by itself. The first stanza, which introduces the comparison of spring to a hand arranging items in a shop window, ends with "and." It is followed by line 9, standing alone on the page: "changing everything carefully." The

Nice introduction. You've stated your topic (enjambment) and also given readers a preview of the poem's theme.

You discuss your examples in the order they appear in the poem, which is a logical way to organize the essay.

Interesting point—the poet places things carefully, just like the spring hand.

1. Analyze   2. Practice   3. Perform

isolation of this line suggests that it is important. It draws the reader's eye to the other single-line stanza at the very end of the poem: "without breaking anything" (19). These may be the most essential ideas about spring that Cummings wants to communicate. Spring changes everything, in a careful way that transforms but does not destroy.

The third stanza opens with the same words from the beginning of the poem, with a couple of interesting differences: "spring is like a perhaps / Hand" (10–11). Here, "spring" is not capitalized, while "Hand" is, suggesting that the speaker is growing more confident in the idea of spring as a hand that arranges things in a purposeful way. The line break also serves to emphasize the hand and its activity. Line 10 ends with "perhaps," but when the reader's eye jumps to the next line, it meets the bold and definite "Hand." Cummings may be pointing out that while spring is careful and does not break anything, it is also a powerful force that cannot be stopped.

A technique like enjambment may not be the first thing one notices when reading a poem. However, with closer analysis, readers can see how the poet uses it to enhance meaning. In "Spring is like a perhaps hand," E. E. Cummings's carefully placed line breaks reinforce his theme about spring— that its changes are subtle but very significant.

I like how you've considered how the poem looks on the page. That was important to Cummings.

Good comparison between line 1 and lines 10–11. The differences are small but meaningful.

Your essay concludes with a strong statement of the poem's overall meaning. Great job!

Works Cited

Cummings, E. E. "Spring is like a perhaps hand." *Complete Poems: 1904–1962.* New York: Liveright Publishing Corporation, 2013. 47. Print.

"The Modernist Poetry of E. E. Cummings." *And Poetry 4 All.* People's Poetry, Inc., Jan. 2015. Web. 20 Mar. 2015.

Discuss and Decide

With a partner, compare the way Atul organized his essay with the way Valerie organized hers. What are the strengths and weaknesses of each approach in helping readers to appreciate the poem?

NOTES

*What effect does irony have
on an audience?*

You will read:

▶ **A BIOGRAPHY**
Mark Antony

▶ **A HISTORICAL NOTE**
Caesar's Death and Shakespeare's Play

▶ **AN INFORMATIONAL TEXT**
What Is . . . Irony in Literature

▶ **A SPEECH**
*Mark Antony's speech
from The Tragedy of Julius Caesar,
Act III. Scene 2.*

You will write:

▶ **A LITERARY ANALYSIS**
*How does Shakespeare use irony in
Mark Antony's speech?*

Source Materials for Step 2

AS YOU READ You will be writing an essay analyzing the use of irony in a famous Shakespearean speech. Carefully study the sources in Step 2. As you read, underline and circle information that may be useful to you when you write your essay.

Source 1: Biography

MARK ANTONY

Along with Julius Caesar, Mark Antony was one of the best-known and most powerful men in Rome in the first century BC. Born in 83 BC to a family that today would be considered middle class, Antony followed in the footsteps of his father, a military commander, and gained his own fame as a cavalry officer after winning important battles for the Roman army.

In 54 BC, Antony was sent to Gaul (the ancient name for France) as an officer for Julius Caesar. The two men forged a friendship that lasted until Caesar's death. As Caesar rose to political power, he saw to it that Antony was chosen for
10   several important positions. In the Republican Civil War, Antony served as Caesar's second in command, and together they defeated other powerful Roman leaders. In 44 BC, Caesar and Antony became co-consuls of Rome, the highest elected officials of the Republic.

One year earlier, the Roman Senate had declared Caesar dictator for life. However, some in the Senate feared that he would become a tyrant and began plotting to have Caesar killed. When rumors of a conspiracy against Caesar started circulating, Mark Antony rushed to alert his friend but was unable to reach him in time. On March 15, 44 BC, Caesar was assassinated. After his funeral oration for Caesar, Antony feared for his own life, so he fled Rome disguised as a slave. However, he soon returned to take
20   charge of Caesar's will. When the will was made public, it revealed that Caesar had left his gardens to the people of Rome and a sum of money to every Roman living in the city. Caesar's will turned the people of Rome against the assassins, since it seemed to prove that Caesar had loved his country.

Source: *Online Guide to Ancient Rome,* **published by The Caesar Club, posted March 15, 2014.**

Discuss and Decide

Think about Mark Antony's relationship with Caesar. What goal might he have had in mind by giving his speech at Caesar's funeral? Cite text evidence in your discussion.

Source 2: Historical Note

Caesar's Death and Shakespeare's Play

Source: *Shakespeare on History* (website of the nonprofit organization Brief Candle).

Shakespeare's play *Julius Caesar* is based on the historical events of 44 BC surrounding the death of Julius Caesar. Caesar, dictator of Rome, had made many enemies during his ascent to power. He was assassinated on March 15 by a group of senators including Brutus, a one-time supporter and friend of Caesar who nonetheless was convinced that the dictator's arrogance and power needed to be stopped.

In the play, Caesar's close friend Mark Antony, in danger himself from the assassins, wants to shift public opinion of Caesar by speaking at his funeral. Antony convinces Brutus that the assassins have nothing to fear from him,
10   so Brutus grants him permission to speak, with four conditions:

- Brutus would speak first.
- Mark Antony would speak immediately afterwards.
- Antony would not blame the conspirators.
- Antony would admit that he spoke with the conspirators' permission.

Brutus does speak first to the people of Rome and explains why he took part in the assassination: "Not that I loved Caesar less, but that I loved Rome more." Brutus presents himself as "an honourable man" who did not want to kill Caesar but needed to destroy Caesar's ambition—his excessive desire for power. He says Caesar's ambitious nature would have led him to enslave the
20   Romans. Then Antony enters with Caesar's body and begins to speak, using Brutus's own words to sway public opinion against the conspirators.

Discuss and Decide

Think about what the assassins have done. Why might Mark Antony believe his life is in danger? Cite text evidence in your discussion.

What Is . . .

Irony in Literature

by Erica Duvall

Irony is a discrepancy or contradiction between what is said and what is meant, or between what happens and what is expected to happen. There are three main kinds of irony in literature.

Situational irony is when an event or situation is not what the audience or the characters would expect. These famous lines from Coleridge's poem "The Rime of the Ancient Mariner" contain a great example: "Water, water, every where, / Nor any drop to drink." When surrounded by water on all sides, as the sailors in the poem are, one would not expect to die of thirst.

Dramatic (or tragic) **irony** occurs when the audience knows something that a character does not. This may be because the audience watched or read about an earlier event that is unknown to the character. For example, in Shakespeare's *Romeo and Juliet,* the audience knows Juliet drank a sleeping potion, but Romeo thinks she is dead. Tragically, he kills himself before she wakes.

Verbal irony is a statement that is intended to mean the opposite of what the words actually say. A character may use irony out of malice, anger, or merely the desire to be witty. Verbal irony can be used in any of the following ways.

- **Humor:** A remark such as "Great job!" when a friend has just done something clumsy is an example of irony used for humorous effect.

- **Sarcasm or satire:** An ironic comment may be used to criticize an idea or to point out a person's flaws (such as hypocrisy or vanity). For example, one might sarcastically say, "I'm so glad we're having liver with onions again for dinner. It's my favorite," when in fact the speaker does not like to eat liver and onions.

1. Analyze 2. Practice 3. Perform

- **Rhetorical device:** An ironic statement can strengthen the force of an argument. This works when the audience recognizes the irony and is thus made to feel even more certain of the opposing "truth." For example, a student running for class president might open his campaign speech by saying, "I know how much everyone loves that we serve liver with onions at the prom each year. And, if elected, I certainly wouldn't make it my very first act in office to change the menu!"

- **Heuristic device:** A heuristic method of arguing leads the audience to discover new ideas and facts through investigation. Verbal irony can be used to lead the audience to conclude that a situation is different from, or not as simple as, what it appears to be. For instance, one might state an idea that one's audience already believes but also present other facts that contradict that idea, with the purpose of guiding them to draw a different conclusion. For example: "I know that we all want the prom menu changed. None of us wants to eat liver with onions. Why should we? We don't need iron to make us strong! So what if a single serving provides 2,000% of the energy-boosting vitamin B-12 that we need to dance all night?"

From *Deep Reading,* November 2013, pages 17–18.

Source 4: Speech

from **The Tragedy of Julius Caesar**, Act III. Scene 2. *by* **William Shakespeare**

After Brutus speaks to the Roman people, Mark Antony enters with Caesar's body and begins to speak.

NOTES

Friends, Romans, countrymen, lend me your ears;
I come to bury Caesar, not to praise him.
The evil that men do lives after them;
The good is oft interred with their bones;
5   So let it be with Caesar. The noble Brutus
Hath told you Caesar was ambitious:
If it were so, it was a grievous fault,
And grievously hath Caesar answer'd it.
Here, under leave of Brutus and the rest,—
10 For Brutus is an honourable man;
So are they all, all honourable men—
Come I to speak in Caesar's funeral.
He was my friend, faithful and just to me:
But Brutus says he was ambitious;
15 And Brutus is an honourable man.
He hath brought many captives home to Rome,
Whose ransoms did the general coffers fill:
Did this in Caesar seem ambitious?
When that the poor have cried, Caesar hath wept:
20 Ambition should be made of sterner stuff:
Yet Brutus says he was ambitious;
And Brutus is an honourable man.
You all did see that on the Lupercal°
I thrice presented him a kingly crown,
25 Which he did thrice refuse: was this ambition?
Yet Brutus says he was ambitious;
And, sure, he is an honourable man.
I speak not to disprove what Brutus spoke,
But here I am to speak what I do know.
30 You all did love him once, not without cause:
What cause withholds you then, to mourn for him?
O judgment! thou art fled to brutish beasts,
And men have lost their reason. Bear with me;
My heart is in the coffin there with Caesar,
35 And I must pause till it come back to me.

From *Julius Caesar* by
William Shakespeare
(London: Iambic Press, 2011),
pages 176–177.

---

23. Lupercal: a.festival honoring Pan

Discuss and Decide

Does Antony follow through with his opening statement? Cite text evidence.

▼

1. Analyze   2. Practice   3. Perform

Respond to Questions on Step 2 Sources

These questions will help you analyze the sources you've read. Use your notes and refer back to the sources in order to answer the questions. Your answers will help you write your essay.

1 **Prose Constructed-Response** In what way was Mark Antony a loyal friend to Caesar? Cite evidence from his biography and at least one other text in your answer.

_____

_____

_____

_____

2 **Prose Constructed-Response** Why do you think Brutus put so many conditions on Antony's speech? What do you think Brutus is afraid of? Cite evidence from Source 2 and at least one other text in your answer.

_____

_____

_____

_____

_____

3 **Prose Constructed-Response** Given the circumstances that surround the speech, why is irony a key tool for Antony to be able to safely achieve his goal? What kinds of irony does he use?

_____

_____

_____

_____

_____

Write a literary analysis that examines Shakespeare's use of irony in Mark Antony's speech from *Julius Caesar*.

Planning and Prewriting

Analyze the Sources

You have read a variety of texts that helped you understand the context of Mark Antony's speech. Think about how this information helped you understand Mark Antony's intentions. In the chart below, cite a fact or detail from each source that helps you analyze the irony in his speech.

Source	Fact or detail	What does this add to my understanding of the irony in Antony's speech?
Biography Mark Antony		
Historical Note Caesar's Death and Shakespeare's Play		
Informational Text Irony in Literature		

1. Analyze   2. Practice   3. Perform

Develop Your Essay

A literary analysis is an examination of a specific aspect of a text. An essayist may put forward an argument or an interpretation of the text.

Determine the Topic

After a thoughtful reading of a text, an essayist chooses one particular aspect to analyze. This becomes the topic of the essay. For the essay you are writing, you are specifically being asked to write on the following topic: Shakespeare's use of irony in Mark Antony's speech in *Julius Caesar*.

Write the Claim or Central Idea

To write the claim or central idea, an essayist puts forward an assertion about the topic and comments upon its importance or significance.

The topic for the model essays in this unit was E. E. Cummings's use of alternate writing conventions in "Spring is like a perhaps hand." Look closely at the ways in which each essayist makes an assertion and comments upon the importance or significance of his or her assertion. In the chart below, identify the assertion that each essayist makes and how the essayist explains the importance or significance of the assertion.

Valerie's Essay
Claim: His free verse poem creates an image of the gradual and uncertain morphing of winter into spring. He explores this familiar theme in his own unique style, with unusual word choices, unexpected line breaks, and odd capitalization and punctuation.
Assertion:
Importance/Significance:

Atul's Essay
Claim: In his poem "Spring is like a perhaps hand," Cummings uses enjambment to support his description of spring as a gentle hand that changes everything around us in gradual, subtle ways that can be hard to perceive.
Assertion:
Importance/Significance:

Using what you have discovered about writing a claim or central idea for a literary analysis, create your own claim for your essay about Mark Antony's speech and write it in the chart on page 97.

Choose the Structure and Craft the Key Points

Essayists choose a structure that aligns to the claim or central idea and for which key points can be pulled from the text. Take a look at the structures chosen by the model essay writers as well as the key points that they crafted.

Valerie's Essay	Atul's Essay
Structure: Four different writing techniques are analyzed.	**Structure:** One writing technique is analyzed in multiple parts of the text.
Key Point 1 – parts of speech	**Key Point 1** – enjambment in lines 2–4 (beginning of poem)
Key Point 2 – enjambment	**Key Point 2** – enjambment in line 9 (middle of poem)
Key Point 3 – capitalization	**Key Point 3** – enjambment in lines 10–11 (end of poem)
Key Point 4 – punctuation	

Using what you have discovered about structure and creating key points, decide on your structure and key points and record them in the following chart.

Topic
Shakespeare's use of irony in Mark Antony's speech in *Julius Caesar*

Claim or Central Idea

Structure and Key Points
(List at least three key points, and more if you need them.)

Structure:

Key Point 1:

Key Point 2:

Key Point 3:

Key Point 4:

Key Point 5:

Collect Textual Evidence

Once an essayist has determined both the structure and the key points, the evidence to support each key point is collected. You can begin to record your evidence in the planner on page 98.

Finalize Your Plan

Organize your key points in an order that makes sense for the analysis. You can address them in order of importance or in the order in which they appear.

▶ Begin with a captivating comment, observation, or question about the reading.

▶ Provide necessary or interesting background information.

▶ Include your central idea.

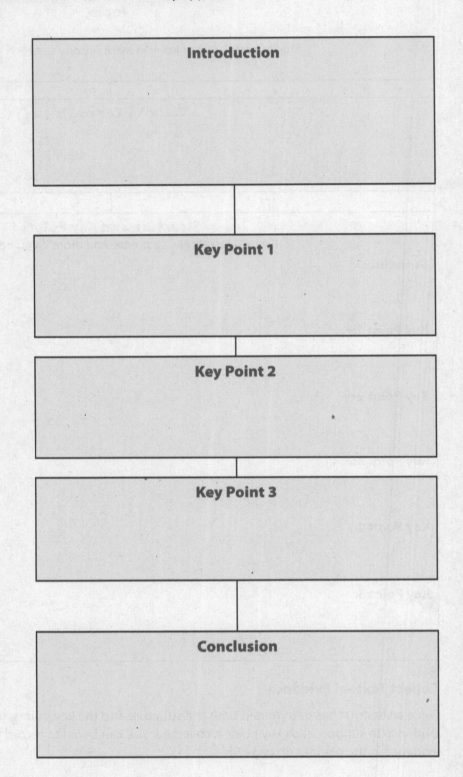

Introduction

▶ State your first key point with support and elaboration.

▶ Develop a separate paragraph for each of your key points, using effective transitions between each one.

▶ Elaborate by explaining how each detail connects to each key point.

Key Point 1

Key Point 2

Key Point 3

▶ Restate your central idea using different words.

▶ Leave your readers with an intriguing thought.

Conclusion

Cite Your Sources

An authoritative literary analysis provides evidence from the literature and from other sources to support the essayist's claim or interpretation. In addition to citing sources, a literary analysis cites specific line numbers from poetry and other verse. The format used by the Modern Language Association (MLA) is demonstrated in the student models on pages 82–85.

Make Notes on Each Source Depending on the exact sources you are using, you'll need to gather certain information to use in your citations. Basic facts include the following:

▶ Author(s)

▶ Title of poem, story, article, or chapter within a longer work

▶ Publication title and type of publication (book, website, magazine, etc.)

▶ Publisher and date of publication

▶ Page numbers, if appropriate—especially for any specific text you plan to quote in your essay

▶ Line numbers for in-text citations of poetry quotations

Place Citations in the Text of Your Essay If you quote lines from prose, use quotation marks to set off the quote. If you paraphrase lines of poetry or prose, no quotation marks are needed. If you quote lines of poetry in your essay, set the lines off with quotation marks and use a slash (/) to indicate line breaks.

In-Text Citation Rules If the sentence or paragraph clearly indicates the name of the author, include only the page number in parentheses at the end of the sentence when quoting from a book, story, or article. Include only the line numbers when quoting from a poem.

> Twain begins the novel with Huck vouching for the accuracy of the story: "There was things which he stretched, but mainly he told the truth" (2).

> In his poem "Mending Wall," Robert Frost writes: "Before I built a wall I'd ask to know / What I was walling in or walling out" (32–33).

If the sentence or paragraph does not clearly indicate the name of the author, include both the author's name and the page number (or line numbers for poetry) in parentheses at the end of the sentence.

> The novel begins with Huck vouching for the accuracy of the story: "There was things which he stretched, but mainly he told the truth" (Twain 2).

> The narrator of "Mending Wall" wonders: "Before I built a wall I'd ask to know / What I was walling in or walling out" (Frost 32–33).

© Houghton Mifflin Harcourt Publishing Company

If you cite more than one text from the same author, provide an abbreviated title for the work to distinguish it from other works. Titles of books or long poems should be underlined or italicized; titles of short stories, short poems, and articles should be set off in quotation marks. See below for two examples of quotations from poems by Robert Frost.

> We see this challenge to the status quo in "Before I built a wall I'd ask to know / What I was walling in or walling out" ("Mending Wall" 32–33).

> "Yet knowing how way leads on to way, / I doubted if I should ever come back" reveals the permanence of decisions ("Road Not Taken" 11–12).

If you are citing from a text with no known author, use a shortened title of the work instead of the author's name and provide a page number.

> "On the pages of books, we embark on quests, discover treasure, and are forever changed without ever leaving the sofa" ("Why Read" 52).

Create Your "Works Cited" List Use the following bulleted points to help organize and format your list:

▶ List all the sources you have used in your essay in a Works Cited list.

▶ Authors are listed with their last names first. The list is then arranged by alphabetical order of the first word in each entry.

▶ Check with your teacher about including URLs for websites, which the MLA considers optional.

▶ Use these guidelines for citing the sources on pages 88–92:

Website	Author(s) (if available). "Title of Page." *Name of Site*. Sponsor or publisher of website (usually an organization or company), date of publication (if available). Medium of publication (Web). Date of access.
Magazine	Author(s). "Title of Article." *Title of Periodical* Day Month Year: pages. Medium of publication (Print, Web, etc.).
Book	Author(s). *Title of Book*. City of publication: Publisher, Year of publication. Medium of publication (Print).

Get Help Online If you have Internet access, citation generators can help you get the format of your Works Cited list just right. Search for "MLA citation generators" or try one of the sites suggested at http://mlaformat.org/mla-format-generator/.

Draft Your Essay

As you write, think about:

▶ **Audience:** Your teacher and classmates

▶ **Purpose:** Demonstrate your understanding of the specific requirements of a literary analysis.

▶ **Style:** Use a formal and objective tone.

▶ **Transitions:** Use words or phrases such as *furthermore* or *in addition* to create cohesion, or flow.

Revise

Revision Checklist: Self Evaluation

Use the checklist below to guide your analysis.

 If you drafted your essay on the computer, you may wish to print it out so that you can more easily evaluate it.

Ask Yourself	Tips	Revision Strategies
1. Does the introduction capture the audience's attention?	Underline the opening question or comment.	Add a question, observation, quote, or background information.
2. Is the central idea clearly stated?	Put parentheses around the central idea.	Rewrite your central idea so that it is clearly stated.
3. Are points presented in a logical order with clear and varied transitions between related ideas?	Identify the logic of the structure, such as order of importance or order of appearance in the literary work. Circle transitions that link the points.	Rearrange body paragraphs to present points in a logical order. Add varied transitions to connect ideas as needed.
4. Is each point illustrated with relevant textual evidence?	Place a star next to each quotation or detail from the text.	Include at least two pieces of supporting evidence for each point, or add more for a stronger analysis.
5. Is there elaboration for each supporting detail?	Put an A next to each key point, a B next to text-evidence details, and a C next to explanation/ interpretation.	Add more text details or more explanation/interpretation of those details.
6. Does the concluding section summarize the essayist's ideas and provide an insight into the author's use of irony?	Place a check mark above the restatement of the essayist's ideas and circle the concluding insight.	Add a summary of key points. Include an insight on the author's use of irony.
7. Are sources cited both within the text and in a Works Cited list?	Highlight specific facts, details, and quotations taken from the literature and other sources.	Add in-text citations as needed. Revise the Works Cited list to correct any formatting errors.

Revision Checklist: Peer Review

Exchange your essay with a classmate, or read it aloud to your partner. As you read and comment on your classmate's essay, focus on logic, organization, and evidence—not on whether you agree with the author's claim. Help each other identify parts of the drafts that need strengthening, reworking, or a new approach.

What To Look For	Notes for My Partner
1. Does the introduction capture the audience's attention?	
2. Is the central idea clearly stated?	
3. Are points presented in a logical order with clear and varied transitions between related ideas?	
4. Is each point illustrated with relevant textual evidence?	
5. Is there elaboration for each supporting detail?	
6. Does the concluding section summarize the essayist's ideas and provide an insight into the effect of the author's use of irony?	
7. Are sources cited within the text and in a Works Cited list?	

Edit

 Edit your essay to correct spelling, grammar, and punctuation errors.

PERFORM THE TASK

How do authors surprise and terrify readers?

You will read:

▶ **AN INFORMATIVE ESSAY**
How Do Horror Writers Create Suspense?

▶ **A SHORT STORY**
"August Heat"

You will write:

▶ **A LITERARY ANALYSIS**
How does W. F. Harvey create suspense in "August Heat"?

Part 1: Read Sources

Source 1: Informative Essay

How Do Horror Writers Create Suspense?

by Percy D'Aco in *Deep Reading*, August 2014 (pages 9–10)

Horror stories are designed to make our pulses race and our skin tingle. They often revolve around mayhem and the stuff of nightmares—death, evil, the demonic, and the like. A great horror story reflects people's deepest fears.

The horror genre has its roots in folk tales and traditional stories, but it did not truly blossom until the 19th century. Some of the most well-known horror tales were written at this time: Bram Stoker's *Dracula*, Mary Shelley's *Frankenstein*, Robert Louis Stevenson's *Strange Case of Dr. Jekyll and Mr. Hyde*, and the short stories of Edgar Allan

10 Poe. These and other 19th-century works have created an enduring legacy for the modern reader and are often reinterpreted and updated as plays, films, and graphic novels.

The characters in horror stories may be realistic like Hannibal Lecter or supernatural like the characters from the *Twilight Saga* series. However, all good horror stories feature a great deal of suspense. Suspense is the uncertainty or anxiety you feel about what will happen next. Writers use several methods to create suspense.

- Foreshadowing is the use of hints to suggest events later in the plot. A horror writer may use foreshadowing to suggest a

20 frightening event that awaits a main character.

© Houghton Mifflin Harcourt Publishing Company • Image Credits: ©Simon Potter/Cultura/Getty Images

© Houghton Mifflin Harcourt Publishing Company

- Writers may create suspense by withholding information from the reader—for instance, how a crime was committed or who committed it. One way to withhold information is to include a narrator who is not trustworthy: He or she may or may not be trying to manipulate the reader.

- Writers create suspense when a character we care about is in peril or must choose between two dangerous courses of action. We read on to find out what will happen next.

30

- A reversal is a sudden change in a character's situation from good to bad or vice versa. For example, someone is enjoying a quiet evening at home when they hear a startling noise in the basement.

The word *suspense* is related to the word *suspended*. When a story keeps us in suspense, we feel almost as if we are suspended in midair. We may even hold our breath without realizing it as we read on eagerly to find out how the story ends.

NOTES

Discuss and Decide

Using other stories or films, gather a collection of examples of each method of creating suspense. In your discussion, be sure to evaluate which precise method is demonstrated in each example.

AUGUST HEAT

by W. F. Harvey

© Houghton Mifflin Harcourt Publishing Company • Image Credits: ©Corbis

AS YOU READ *Focus on the way the writer creates suspense. Note which methods build tension throughout the story.*

NOTES

Phenistone Road, Clapham, August 20, 190—.

I have had what I believe to be the most remarkable day in my life, and while the events are still fresh in my mind, I wish to put them down on paper as clearly as possible.

Let me say at the outset that my name is James Clarence Withencroft.

I am forty years old, in perfect health, never having known a day's illness.

By profession I am an artist, not a very successful one, but I earn
10   enough money by my black-and-white work to satisfy my necessary wants.

My only near relative, a sister, died five years ago, so that I am independent.

I breakfasted this morning at nine, and after glancing through the morning paper I lighted my pipe and proceeded to let my mind wander in the hope that I might chance upon some subject for my pencil.

The room, though door and windows were open, was oppressively hot, and I had just made up my mind that the coolest and most comfortable place in the neighborhood would be the deep end of the
20   public swimming bath, when the idea came.

I began to draw. So intent was I on my work that I left my lunch untouched, only stopping work when the clock of St. Jude's struck four.

The final result, for a hurried sketch, was, I felt sure, the best thing I had done.

From *Creepy Stories* (Milwaukee: Turkey Creek Books, 2009), pages 92–97.

1. Analyze   2. Practice   3. Perform

It showed a criminal in the dock immediately after the judge had pronounced sentence. The man was fat—enormously fat. The flesh hung in rolls about his chin; it creased his huge, stumpy neck. He was clean shaven (perhaps I should say a few days before he must have been clean shaven) and almost bald. He stood in the dock, his short, stumpy fingers clasping the rail, looking straight in front of him. The feeling that his expression conveyed was not so much one of horror as of utter, absolute collapse.

There seemed nothing in the man strong enough to sustain that mountain of flesh.

I rolled up the sketch, and without quite knowing why, placed it in my pocket. Then with the rare sense of happiness which the knowledge of a good thing well done gives, I left the house.

I believe that I set out with the idea of calling upon Trenton, for I remember walking along Lytton Street and turning to the right along Gilchrist Road at the bottom of the hill where the men were at work on the new tram lines.

From there onward I have only the vaguest recollections of where I went. The one thing of which I was fully conscious was the awful heat, that came up from the dusty asphalt pavement as an almost palpable wave. I longed for the thunder promised by the great banks of copper-colored cloud that hung low over the western sky.

I must have walked five or six miles, when a small boy roused me from my reverie by asking the time.

It was twenty minutes to seven.

When he left me I began to take stock of my bearings. I found myself standing before a gate that led into a yard bordered by a strip of thirsty earth, where there were flowers, purple stock and scarlet geranium. Above the entrance was a board with the inscription—

CHAS. ATKINSON

MONUMENTAL MASON

WORKER IN ENGLISH AND ITALIAN MARBLES

From the yard itself came a cheery whistle, the noise of hammer blows, and the cold sound of steel meeting stone.

Discuss and Decide

With a small group, discuss your impression of the narrator. Is he trustworthy? Cite text evidence in your discussion.

NOTES

A sudden impulse made me enter.

60 A man was sitting with his back toward me, busy at work on a slab of curiously veined marble. He turned round as he heard my steps and stopped short.

It was the man I had been drawing, whose portrait lay in my pocket.

He sat there, huge and elephantine, the sweat pouring from his scalp, which he wiped with a red silk handkerchief. But though the face was the same, the expression was absolutely different.

He greeted me smiling, as if we were old friends, and shook my hand.

I apologized for my intrusion.

70 "Everything is hot and glary outside," I said. "This seems an oasis in the wilderness."

" I don't know about the oasis," he replied, "but it certainly is hot, as hot as hell. Take a seat, sir!"

He pointed to the end of the gravestone on which he was at work, and I sat down.

"That's a beautiful piece of stone you've got hold of," I said.

He shook his head. "In a way it is," he answered; "the surface here is as fine as anything you could wish, but there's a big flaw at the back, though I don't expect you'd ever notice it. I could never make really a

80 good job of a bit of marble like that. It would be all right in the summer like this; it wouldn't mind the blasted heat. But wait till the winter comes. There's nothing like frost to find out the weak points in stone."

"Then what's it for?" I asked.

The man burst out laughing.

"You'd hardly believe me if I was to tell you it's for an exhibition, but it's the truth. Artists have exhibitions; so do grocers and butchers; we have them too. All the latest little things in headstones, you know."

He went on to talk of marbles, which sort best withstood wind and rain, and which were easiest to work; then of his garden and a new sort

90 of carnation he had bought. At the end of every other minute he would drop his tools, wipe his shining head, and curse the heat.

I said little, for I felt uneasy. There was something unnatural, uncanny, in meeting this man.

I tried at first to persuade myself that I had seen him before, that his face, unknown to me, had found a place in some out-of-the-way corner of my memory, but I knew that I was practicing little more than a plausible piece of self-deception.

Mr. Atkinson finished his work, spat on the ground, and got up with a sigh of relief.

100 "There! What do you think of that?" he said, with an air of evident pride.

The inscription which I read for the first time was this—

SACRED TO THE MEMORY

OF

JAMES CLARENCE WITHENCROFT

BORN JAN. 18TH, 1860

HE PASSED AWAY VERY SUDDENLY

ON AUGUST 20TH, 190—

"In the midst of life we are in death."

110 For some time I sat in silence. Then a cold shudder ran down my spine. I asked him where he had seen the name.

"Oh, I didn't see it anywhere," replied Mr. Atkinson. "I wanted some name, and I put down the first that came into my head. Why do you want to know?"

"It's a strange coincidence, but it happens to be mine."
He gave a long, low whistle.

"And the dates?"

"I can only answer for one of them, and that's correct."

"It's a rum go!" he said.

120 But he knew less than I did. I told him of my morning's work. I took the sketch from my pocket and showed it to him. As he looked, the expression of his face altered until it became more and more like that of the man I had drawn.

"And it was only the day before yesterday," he said, "that I told Maria there were no such things as ghosts!"

Neither of us had seen a ghost, but I knew what he meant.

"You probably heard my name," I said.

"And you must have seen me somewhere and have forgotten it!

Discuss and Decide

With a small group, identify three methods of suspense that are found in this story and cite text evidence that illustrates each method.

Were you at Clacton-on-Sea last July?"

130   I had never been to Clacton in my life. We were silent for some time. We were both looking at the same thing, the two dates on the gravestone, and one was right.

     "Come inside and have some supper," said Mr. Atkinson.

     His wife was a cheerful little woman, with the flaky red cheeks of the country-bred. Her husband introduced me as a friend of his who was an artist. The result was unfortunate, for after the sardines and watercress had been removed, she brought me out a Doré Bible, and I had to sit and express my admiration for nearly half an hour.

     I went outside, and found Atkinson sitting on the gravestone

140 smoking.

     We resumed the conversation at the point we had left off.

     "You must excuse my asking," I said, "but do you know of anything you've done for which you could be put on trial?"

     He shook his head.

     "I'm not a bankrupt, the business is prosperous enough. Three years ago I gave turkeys to some of the guardians at Christmas, but that's all I can think of. And they were small ones, too," he added as an afterthought.

     He got up, fetched a can from the porch, and began to water the

150 flowers. "Twice a day regular in the hot weather," he said, "and then the heat sometimes gets the better of the delicate ones. And ferns, good Lord! They could never stand it. Where do you live?"

© Houghton Mifflin Harcourt Publishing Company • Image Credits: ©Corbis

I told him my address. It would take an hour's quick walk to get back home.

"It's like this," he said. "We'll look at the matter straight. If you go back home to-night, you take your chance of accidents. A cart may run over you, and there's always banana skins and orange peel, to say nothing of fallen ladders."

He spoke of the improbable with an intense seriousness that would
160 have been laughable six hours before. But l did not laugh.

"The best thing we can do," he continued, "is for you to stay here till twelve o'clock. We'll go upstairs and smoke; it may be cooler inside.'

To my surprise, I agreed.

We are sitting in a long, low room beneath the eaves. Atkinson has sent his wife to bed. He himself is busy sharpening some tools at a little oilstone, smoking one of my cigars the while.

The air seems charged with thunder. I am writing this at a shaky table before the open window. The leg is cracked, and Atkinson, who seems a handy man with his tools, is going to mend it as soon as he has
170 finished putting an edge on his chisel.

It is after eleven now. I shall be gone in less than an hour.

But the heat is stifling.

It is enough to send a man mad.

Close Read

What do you think is going to happen to the narrator? Which method of suspense is being employed in this ending? Cite text evidence in your response.

_____

_____

_____

_____

Respond to Questions on Step 3 Sources

These questions will help you think about the informational essay and the short story that you have read. Use your notes and refer to the sources in order to answer the questions. Your answers to these questions will help you write your essay.

1 **Prose Constructed-Response** What is mysterious about the events in lines 50–63? Cite specific evidence from the text.

_____

_____

_____

_____

2 **Prose Constructed-Response** What events in the story does the author foreshadow? What clues hint at these events? Cite text evidence in your response.

_____

_____

_____

_____

_____

3 **Prose Constructed-Response** How does the ending create a frightening effect? Cite text evidence in your response.

_____

_____

_____

_____

Part 2: Write

ASSIGNMENT

Write a literary analysis that answers this question: How does W. F. Harvey create suspense in "August Heat"?

Plan

Use the graphic organizer to help you outline the structure of your literary analysis.

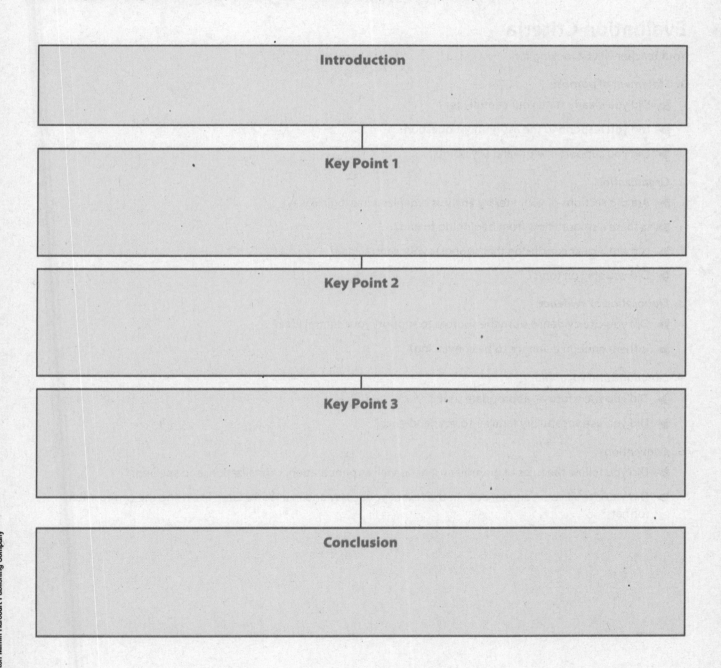

Introduction

Key Point 1

Key Point 2

Key Point 3

Conclusion

Draft

 Use your notes and completed graphic organizer to write a first draft of your literary analysis.

Revise and Edit

 Look back over your essay and compare it to the Evaluation Criteria. Revise your literary analysis and edit it to correct spelling, grammar, and punctuation errors.

Evaluation Criteria

Your teacher will be looking for:

1. *Statement of purpose*
   ▶ Did you clearly state your central idea?
   ▶ Did you respond to the assignment question?
   ▶ Did you support it with valid key points?

2. *Organization*
   ▶ Are the sections of your literary analysis organized in a logical way?
   ▶ Is there a smooth flow from beginning to end?
   ▶ Is there a clear conclusion that supports your central idea?
   ▶ Did you stay on topic?

3. *Elaboration of evidence*
   ▶ Did you cite evidence from the sources to support your central idea?
   ▶ Is there enough evidence to be convincing?

4. *Language and vocabulary*
   ▶ Did you use a formal, appropriate tone?
   ▶ Did you use vocabulary familiar to your audience?

5. *Conventions*
   ▶ Did you follow the rules of grammar usage as well as punctuation, capitalization, and spelling?
   ▶ Did you cite all your sources, both in the text of your essay and in a Works Cited list, using the correct MLA formats?

On Your Own

Time Management: Argumentative Task

TASK 1

RESEARCH SIMULATION

Argumentative Essay

Your Assignment

You will read two texts about keeping exotic animals as pets. Then you will write an argumentative essay in which you take a position on the topic.

Time Management: Argumentative Task

There are two parts to most formal writing tests. Both parts of the tests are timed, so it's important to use your limited time wisely.

Part 1: Read Sources

Preview the articles as you check how many pages you will be reading. This will give you an overview of the contents and help you identify important information.

This is a lot to do in a short time.

Preview the Assignment

35 minutes

You will have 35 minutes to read several articles about private citizens keeping exotic animals as pets. You will then write an essay on the topic.

35 minutes! That's not much time.

How many?

How many pages of reading?

How do you plan to use the 35 minutes?

Underline, circle, and take notes as you read. You probably won't have time to reread.

Estimated time to read:
  "Do You Really Want a Baby Tiger?"   minutes

Estimated time to read:
  "REXANO Proves Politicians and Lobbyists..."   minutes

Total   35   minutes

Any concerns?

_____

_____

_____

_____

_____

_____

_____

Part 2: Write the Essay

85

How much time do you have? Pay attention to the clock!

Plan and Write an Argumentative Essay

→ 85 minutes

You will have 85 minutes to plan, write, revise, and edit your essay.

Your Plan

Before you start to write, decide on your precise claim. Then think about the evidence you will use to support your claim.

How do you plan to use the 85 minutes?

Be sure to leave enough time for this step.

Estimated time for planning the essay?	____ minutes
Estimated time for writing?	____ minutes
Estimated time for revising?	____ minutes
Estimated time for editing, including checking spelling, grammar, and punctuation?	____ minutes
Total	**85 minutes**

Notes:

_____

_____

_____

_____

_____

Reread your essay, making sure that the points are clear. Check that there are no spelling or punctuation mistakes.

▶ Your Assignment

You will read several articles and then write an argumentative essay that takes a precise position regarding keeping exotic animals as pets.

Complete the following steps as you compose your essay.

1. Read an article about owning exotic pets.

2. Read an article from a group that supports owners of exotic animals.

3. Plan, write, and revise your essay.

▶ Part 1 (35 minutes)

As you read the sources, take notes on important facts and details. You may want to refer to your notes while planning and writing your essay.

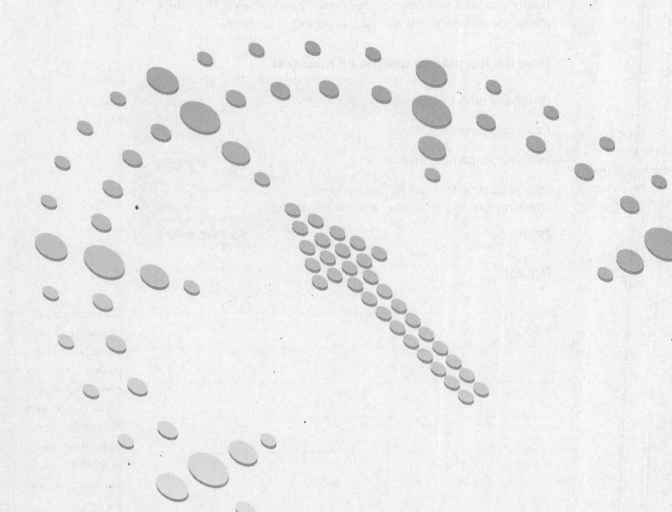

Do You Really Want a
Baby Tiger?

Second thoughts about owning an exotic pet

by Mia Lewis from *SmartPet.com*. Petscorp International, 2012.

© Houghton Mifflin Harcourt Publishing Company

NOTES

You know the story: Jenny wants a puppy, but her parents are reluctant to take the plunge. They remind her of the responsibilities that go along with pet ownership: She'll have to take it for a walk, every day, no matter what; it'll grow up from the cute puppy it is now to a gnarly old dog; there will be messes to clean up, food to buy, and trips to the vet. Jenny says she doesn't mind any of that, and soon Fido is welcomed into the family fold. In no time at all the parents love Fido just as much as Jenny does, and Fido loves them all back. It is a story with a happy ending.

10   But what if Jenny tried to persuade her parents to buy her a fuzzy lion cub she saw advertised, or a baby chimpanzee? If they had any sense, Jenny's parents would tell her "No way" and stick to their guns. Owning an exotic pet is expensive, time consuming, and a huge responsibility. And of course, it can be dangerous. Owning a wild animal is arguably cruel to the animal in a way that owning a domestic animal isn't. Given all these considerations, it's remarkable how many people decide to become owners of exotic pets.

For some, the allure of owning an exotic pet trumps any drawbacks. After all, it's not your average Joe who owns a python, or a puff adder! A house with a monkey or lion cub in the backyard
20   is going to stand out in the neighborhood. No one will deny that owning an exotic pet is daring and different. But many experts argue that the negatives strongly outweigh the benefits. Here's a look at some of the reasons why owning an exotic animal as a pet is NOT such a good idea.

They all grow up. A cute puppy grows up to be a dog—bigger, but not dangerously so. A lion cub, on the other hand, inevitably turns into, well, a lion. Most people who own exotic pets find them irresistible—and manageable—when they are small. But an adorable
30   cub becomes a powerful adult soon enough. Many exotic animals

are strong enough to be dangerous even without meaning to cause harm. An adult animal is also likely to be aggressive and have more difficult behaviors than a baby one.

Wild animals are wild, even in captivity. A dog is an animal, but it is a *domesticated* one—a species that has evolved over thousands of years to live well with people. Most dogs can be trained with a few puppy obedience classes. Exotic animals are something else entirely. They are wild animals with wild animal instincts, even when born in captivity. A wild animal is never 100 percent predictable. An animal that has behaved one way for many years cannot suddenly change. Domestication is not something that happens in one or two generations: it takes hundreds or thousands of years.

Do you really have the resources? If keeping a dog or cat can be time consuming and costly, that's nothing compared to looking after an adult lion or chimpanzee. It's not just the food and the vet bills, although those can indeed be considerable. You also have to build a sturdy cage or enclosure that is the appropriate size and has the right hiding, resting, climbing, and play spaces to approximate the animal's natural habitat. You will need to be able to devote a large portion of your time to learning about the animal and its needs. Usually only specially trained and qualified individuals working with the backing of a specially equipped facility are fully able to meet the needs of exotic animals. Keep in mind that pet ownership is a lifetime commitment. Jenny's dog may live to be 15, but a chimpanzee can live to be 60 or 65 years old.

Dangers and Diseases. While it is true that even dogs and cats can injure their owners or other people, they do not have the same unpredictable potential for serious or even deadly attacks that many exotic pets do. It's not just big cats, poisonous snakes, and chimpanzees that can be harmful—even smaller exotic pets can cause serious injuries. Exotic pets can also spread diseases to humans. In addition, many exotic pets end up on the loose in the wild. (Owners who find their fully-grown pets unmanageable sometimes release them.) Out on their own, these exotic animals can be a further danger to the public, and even to the environment.

Cruel and Unusual. Many exotic pet owners end up being unable to provide the proper living environment for their fully-grown pets. In order to prevent them from injuring anyone, they may
70 decide to keep them caged. The end result is that far too many of these exotic animals spend almost their entire lives in the "prison" of a small cage. In this kind of environment, they have no opportunity to practice most of their natural behaviors.

All in all, Jenny is better off sticking with a "boring" dog or cat. If I were her parents, I'd say yes to the puppy before she got any more "exotic" ideas!

NOTES

Am I on Track?

Actual Time Spent Reading

REXANO Proves Politicians and Lobbyists Introducing and Passing Laws Against Exotic Animal Ownership in the Name of 'Public Safety' Use False and Misleading Claims

from *PRWeb*. Rexano, 17 March 2007.

Private owners of wild and exotic animals in the USA have been coming under ever increasing attacks from animal rights (AR) activists and uninformed legislators to end the private ownership of exotics in the name of "public safety." Many unfair laws have already passed on the federal, state and local levels.

REXANO (Responsible Exotic Animal Ownership), a free web resource designed to give facts-based research material to private owners of exotics to fight unfair legislation, just finished compiling a statistical table proving the legislators passing laws under the guise of

10 public safety used misleading claims.

"In the last 10–16 years, 1.5 people on average gets killed yearly by captive reptile, 1 by captive big cat, 0.81 by captive elephant, 0.125 by captive bear and 0 by captive nonhuman primate," reports Zuzana Kukol, a REXANO co-founder. "As a comparison, 45,000 people die each year in traffic accidents, 47 from lightning and 1,600 by falling down stairs."

"Our statistical analysis of the data disproves the claim that exotic animals in captivity are a threat to public safety. No uninvolved public has ever been killed in the USA since 1990 as a

20 result of a captive big cat, primate, bear, elephant or reptile at large," adds Scott Shoemaker, a REXANO co-founder. "The majority of fatalities are to owners, trainers or people voluntarily visiting the property where the animals are kept."

"If it is illegal for businesses to advertise and sell products using misleading and fraudulent claims, why is it OK for legislators and lobbyists to introduce, gain public support and pass bills using fraudulent claims they can't back up with facts?" asks Kukol. "These bills that waste tax money are appeasing the minority of special interest animal rights groups and a few individuals falling for the

30 claims of imaginary threat at the expense of constitutional freedoms for a majority of Americans. Many animal businesses are regulated out of existence as a result of this deception."

"There are no hard facts and statistics to support the case for these bans, only so-called incident reports compiled by the various AR groups," says Andrew Wyatt, President of NC Association of Reptile Keepers. "These incident reports amount to scary stories about scary animals. Many are unconfirmed, manufactured or ridiculous. Deaths or serious injuries are exceedingly rare. The reality is that you are more likely to contract *E. coli* virus from eating

40   spinach, and die as a result, than die from being attacked by an exotic animal."

"It would be nice if for once the AR fanatics could refrain from exploiting isolated tragic incidents, but they never do. They feed on this kind of hysteria," says Feline Conservation Federation president Lynn Culver. "AR groups use grieving relatives of those harmed by exotic animals as their poster children to help push their agenda of prohibiting exotic animals in society."

"Fear trumps over freedom. Will America be coerced by inflammatory rhetoric from the AR Movement into over reacting to

50   a nonexistent threat by enacting overly intrusive animal bans? I hope not," adds Wyatt.

"Animals are personal property; and we oppose legislation that restricts the private ownership or use of animals, or that inhibits free trade of any animal provided it meets Ohio Department of Agriculture testing and import requirements," adds Polly Britton, Secretary of the Ohio Association of Animal Owners.

"As long as animal welfare and public safety laws are followed, the private ownership of all animals should be protected in the USA," says Shoemaker.

60   "Control the land and the animals, then you control the people," states Kim Bloomer a natural pet care educator, lecturer and host of the online radio show Animal Talk Naturally.

"There is a hidden agenda with regard to all of these laws and it has nothing to do with public safety or concerns for good animal care. Rather, it is about eroding or removing American freedoms, the right to own as many animals as we can provide for."

Current focus of REXANO is to reverse the trend in over regulation.

Am I on Track?

Actual Time Spent Reading

▶ Part 2 (85 minutes)

You now have 85 minutes to review your notes and sources, and to plan, draft, revise, and edit your essay. While you may use your notes and refer to the sources, your essay must represent your original work. Now read your assignment and begin your work.

Your assignment

You have read two texts about keeping exotic animals as pets.

• "Do You Really Want a Baby Tiger?"

• "REXANO Proves Politicians and Lobbyists..."

Consider the information presented about owning exotic pets in each text.

Write an essay that explains your position on owning exotic pets. Remember to use textual evidence to support your claim.

Now begin work on your essay. Manage your time carefully so that you can:

1. plan your essay

2. write your essay

3. revise and edit your final draft

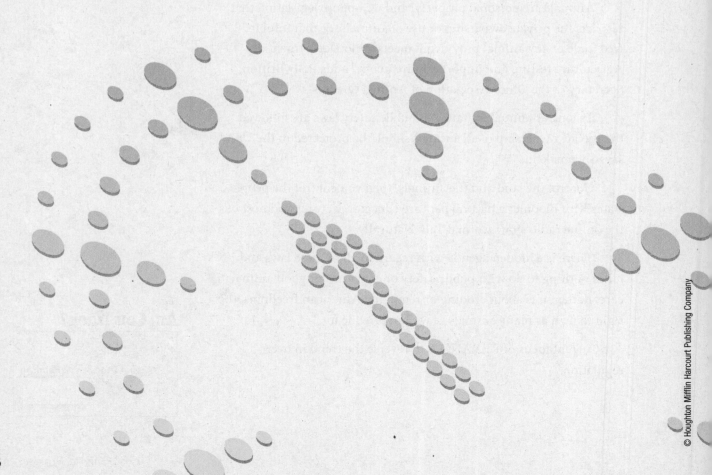

RESEARCH SIMULATION

Informative Essay

Your Assignment
You will read two essays on the importance of communication while hiking. Then you will write an informative essay about why it is important to communicate your whereabouts when going on an outdoor excursion.

Time Management: Informative Task

There are two parts to most formal writing tests. Both parts of the tests are timed, so it's important to use your limited time wisely.

Part 1: Read Sources

Preview the Assignment

35 minutes

You will have 35 minutes to read two selections about hiking outdoors. You will then write an essay on the topic.

How many?

How many pages of reading?

How do you plan to use the 35 minutes?

Estimated time to read:
  "Miraculous Lost and Found" _____ minutes

Estimated time to read:
  "The Most Important Rule" _____ minutes

Total   **35**   **minutes**

Any concerns?

_____

_____

_____

_____

_____

_____

_____

Preview the selections. This will help you get an overview of the contents and let you identify important information.

This is a lot to do in a short time.

35 minutes! That's not much time.

Underline, circle, and take notes as you read. You probably won't have time to reread.

Part 2: Write the Essay

85

How much time do you have? Pay attention to the clock!

Plan and Write an Informative Essay

85 minutes

You will have 85 minutes to plan, write, revise, and edit your essay.

Your Plan

Before you start writing, think about the central idea of your essay. What is the most important point you need to make?

_____

_____

How do you plan to use the 85 minutes?

Estimated time for planning the essay?		minutes
Estimated time for writing?		minutes
Estimated time for revising?		minutes
Estimated time for editing, including checking spelling, grammar and punctuation?		minutes
Total	**85**	**minutes**

Be sure to leave enough time for this step.

Notes:

_____

_____

_____

_____

Reread your essay, making sure that the points are clear. Check that there are no spelling or punctuation mistakes.

▶ Your Assignment

> You will read two articles about hiking alone and then write an informative essay about the importance of communicating your whereabouts when going on an outdoor excursion.

Complete the following steps as you plan and compose your essay.

1. Read a news article about a man who became trapped by a boulder when hiking alone.

2. Read an article about rules to follow when hiking.

3. Plan, write, and revise your essay.

▶ Part 1 (35 minutes)

As you read the sources, take notes on important facts and details. You may want to refer to your notes while planning and writing your essay.

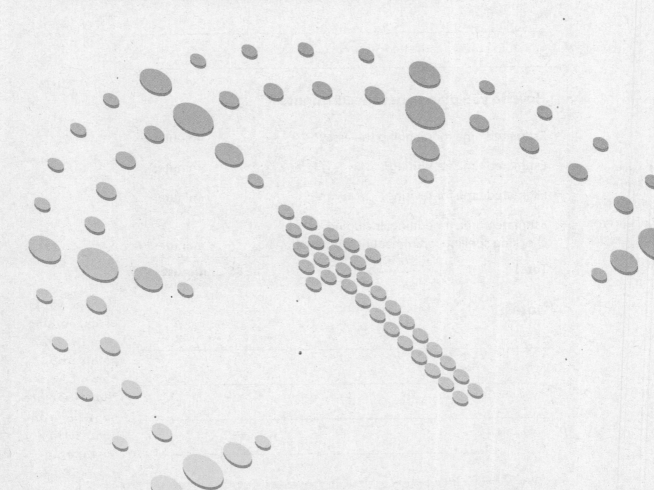

THE WAYNE COUNTY GAZETTE

Miraculous Lost and Found

by Katherine Leonard, *Staff Writer*   *Friday, May 2, 2003*

Aron Ralston, a mountaineer from Aspen, Colorado, lost for over five days in Blue John Canyon, was miraculously found alive yesterday. The experienced climber had been trapped by a big boulder that came loose and pinned his arm against the wall of a narrow canyon that he was descending. Ralston was able to free himself by amputating his arm with a multi-tool pocket knife.

The Meijers, a Dutch family that was hiking in the park, saw Ralston walking aimlessly a few hours after he performed the amputation. They gave him food and water, and alerted a rescue
10 team that was already in the area looking for the missing climber.

The authorities are putting together the pieces that form this incredible survival story as more details of Ralston's ordeal surface. It seems that the Colorado climber was mountain-biking in the Canyonlands National Park when he put down his bike to take a closer look at a very narrow canyon. As he was climbing down, the boulder, with a reported weight of 800 pounds, broke loose and, rolling down, got stuck, pinning Ralston's arm against the wall. Ralston had not told anyone where he was going, or when he expected to return, making a disastrous situation much, much worse.

20 Slowly consuming the only food he had to eat, two burritos, and taking small sips of his remaining water (about 350 ml), the mountaineer spent the majority of four days waiting for somebody to find him. On his fourth night, he is said to have had an epiphany— amputation was his only way to survive. No one knew he was missing. He would have to rescue himself.

Ralston spent several hours using a dull knife to cut his own arm at the radius. Once free, he rappelled down a 65-foot wall with one hand and started walking the 8 miles to his car. It was then the Meijer family found him and got help. Ralston was taken
30 to a hospital in Grand Junction, Co., where he remains in critical condition. "He was in pretty rough shape but he communicated with us all the way to the hospital," said the Emery County sheriff Mitch Vetere. "He is obviously a tough guy." Ralston had lost 40 pounds and quite a bit of blood by the time he got to the hospital.

Am I on Track?

Actual Time Spent Reading

ANCHOR TEXT

The Most Important Rule

by Jared Myers in *Going Outdoors*. Ed. Claude Wolverhamton. Seattle: Woodsworks, 2015. 31–32.

As any good adventurist knows, there are a number of common-sense rules to follow when engaging in a successful hike: bring plenty of water, dress appropriately, map out the trail you will be hiking in advance, and be sure to bring along a first aid kit. However, the most important rule of hiking is also one of the most commonly overlooked: Alert a family member or friend to the location of your proposed hike and an estimated time of return.

While any amount of advance planning or familiarity with a particular hiking trail may seem to be an adequate substitute for alerting a friend or loved one, rarely does this planning or familiarity account for an emergency. These unexpected difficulties can come in many forms, including swiftly deteriorating weather conditions, an encounter with dangerous wildlife, or even something as small as a sprained ankle.

For example, in an effort to follow in the footsteps of hiker Aron Ralston, 64-year-old Amos Wayne Richards made an attempt to traverse Utah's Blue John Canyon in September of 2011. However, after falling 10 feet, Richards dislocated his shoulder and shattered his leg. With only two protein bars, an empty water bottle, no family or friends aware of his hiking plans, and no cell phone service with which to contact them, Richards began to drag himself back to his car along the rocky terrain. Four days later, rangers set off to rescue him, tipped off by the discovery of his abandoned campsite and truck. From clues at the campsite and from conversations with Richards's family and friends, rangers figured out where he was likely located and dispatched a helicopter. After using the flash on his camera to catch the attention of the pilot, Amos Wayne Richards was treated for his broken leg and for dehydration at a nearby hospital before being released. The whole ordeal, however, could have been prevented, had he simply informed a friend or family member of his hiking plans and his estimated time of return.

New advancements in technology have made it easier for hikers to plan for unexpected emergencies in advance, without worrying their friends and family unnecessarily. HikerAlert, a web-based

service, allows you to enter your hiking itinerary and projected return time into its database before your departure. If you fail to respond to a text from the HikerAlert website, checking in with you at your projected return time, a text is sent to your designated emergency contacts entered when the account was created,
40 encouraging them to attempt to contact you.

It's easy to understand why someone may feel it unnecessary to reach out to friends and family before going out on a new adventure. For some, admitting the possibility of danger may make them feel that they appear to be weak or inexperienced. Others may feel that their friends or family may worry too much about them while they are away. However, following this one simple rule may ultimately save your life and ensure that the next hike you go on won't be your last.

Am I on Track?

Actual Time Spent Reading

▶ Part 2 (85 minutes)

You now have 85 minutes to review your notes and sources, and to plan, draft, revise, and edit your essay. While you may use your notes and refer to the sources, your work must represent your original work. Now read your assignment and begin your work.

Your assignment

You have read two texts about hiking alone.

• "Miraculous Lost and Found"

• "The Most Important Rule"

Consider the information presented about the dangers of hiking alone.

Write an essay that explains why it is important to communicate your destination when hiking alone. Remember to use textual evidence to support your claim.

Now begin work on your essay. Manage your time carefully so that you can:

1. plan your essay

2. write your essay

3. revise and edit your final draft

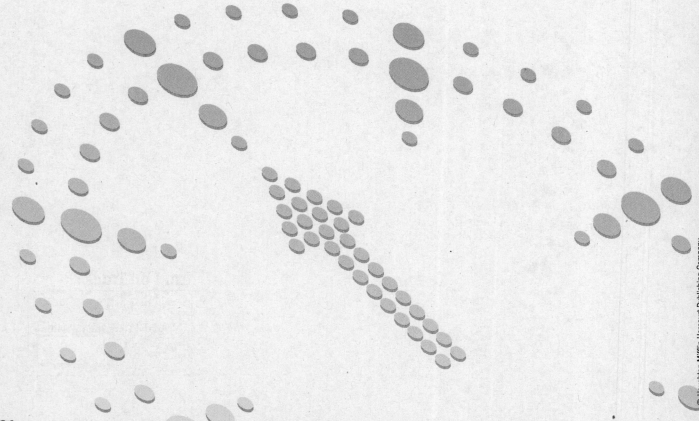

TASK 3

Literary Analysis

Your Assignment

You will read two informational essays about Edgar Allan Poe and his famous poem "The Raven." Then you will write a literary analysis of Poe's poem.

Time Management: Literary Analysis Task

Most formal writing tests are made up of two parts. Both parts of the tests are timed, so it's important to use your limited time wisely.

Part 1: Read Sources

Preview the Assignment

35 minutes

You will have 35 minutes to read two essays and the famous poem "The Raven" by Edgar Allan Poe. You will then write a prose constructed-response using the sources.

35 minutes! That's not much time.

Preview the materials. This will give you an overview of the contents and help you identify important ideas and details.

How many?

How many pages of reading? ⬜

How many prose constructed-response questions? ⬜

How do you plan to use the 35 minutes?

Underline, circle, and take notes as you read. You probably won't have time to reread.

Estimated time to read:

"Edgar Allan Poe" ⬜ minutes

"The Raven" ⬜ minutes

"Poe's Process: Writing 'The Raven'" ⬜ minutes

This is a lot to do in a short time.

Estimated time to write prose constructed-response? ⬜ minutes

Total   35   **minutes**

Any concerns?

_____

_____

_____

_____

Part 2: Write the Analysis

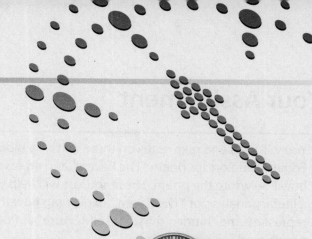

85

How much time do you have? Pay attention to the clock! →

Plan and Write a Literary Analysis

85 minutes

You will have 85 minutes to plan, write, revise, and edit your literary analysis.

Your Plan

Before you start writing, decide how you will structure your literary analysis.

How do you plan to use the 85 minutes?

Estimated time for planning the essay?		minutes
Estimated time for writing?		minutes
Estimated time for revising?		minutes
Estimated time for editing, including checking spelling, grammar and punctuation?		minutes
Total	**85**	**minutes**

Be sure to leave enough time for this step. →

Notes:

_____

_____

_____

_____

_____

Reread your essay, making sure that the points are clear. Check that there are no spelling or punctuation mistakes.

▶ Your Assignment

> You will read and take notes on three texts—a biography of Edgar Allan Poe, his poem "The Raven," and an essay about how Poe wrote the poem. These sources will help you write a literary analysis of "The Raven," explaining how the poem represents the "human thirst for self-torture" as Poe himself proclaimed.

Complete the following steps as you plan and compose your essay.

1. Read a short biography of Edgar Allan Poe.

2. Read the poem "The Raven" by Edgar Allan Poe.

3. Read an essay titled "Poe's Process: Writing 'The Raven.'"

4. Write a prose constructed-response.

5. Plan, write, and revise your essay.

▶ Part 1 (35 minutes)

As you read the sources, take notes on important facts and details. You may want to refer to your notes while planning and writing your essay.

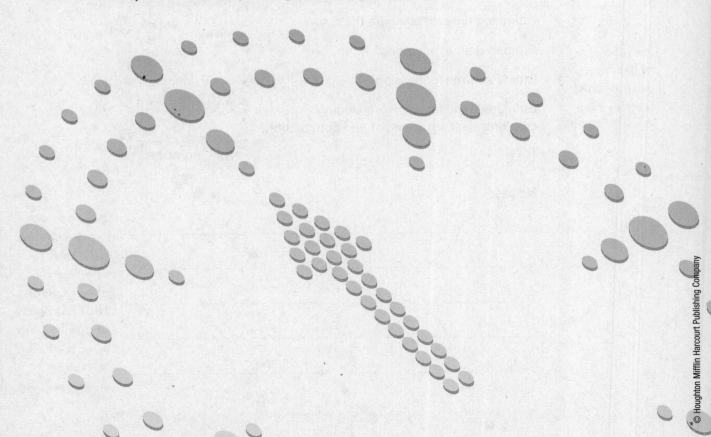

© Houghton Mifflin Harcourt Publishing Company

BIOGRAPHY

Edgar Allan Poe

by Lynn Malle in *The Poe We Know.* Ed. Angela Gordon-Pimm. Baltimore: Charm City Press, 2010. 45–46.

NOTES

The author of "The Raven," which numbers among the best-known poems in American literature, Edgar Allan Poe (c. 1809–1849) was a master of the horror tale and the psychological thriller. His tales of the gruesome and grotesque contain distraught narrators, mentally deranged heroes, and doomed heroines. His stories and poems, steeped in Gothic horror, move beyond the rational world to explore the dark, irrational depths of the human mind. A poet, literary critic, and an innovator of fiction, Poe was once called one of

10 literature's "most brilliant, but erratic, stars."

Well known for his unstable life and for his formidable talent, Poe was abandoned by his father as an infant. Tragically, he lost his mother to tuberculosis when he was three and was taken in by John Allan, a wealthy Virginia businessman. However, Allan and he had a stormy relationship, and at age 18, Poe was forced to leave due to financial difficulty, thus beginning a lifelong pattern of self-destruction. Estranged from Allan as a young man, Poe formed a new family with his aunt and his young cousin, Virginia Clemm, whom he married

20 when she was only 13 or 14, probably marrying her secretly and then publicly a year later, in 1836. Unfortunately, Virginia died 11 years after their marriage, and Poe, who was devastated by her death, died two years later.

For much of his adult life, Poe struggled to support his family. He landed promising positions at several literary magazines, spoiling one opportunity after another with his erratic behavior. At the same time, his scathing reviews made him a feared and respected literary critic, and his inventive short stories brought him fame as a fiction writer. Although

30 his life matched the romantic ideal of the starving artist who suffered for the purity of his art, Poe's stories were designed to reach a large audience. His success with horror, science fiction, and detective stories proved his mastery of popular genres.

Poe's distinctive themes included madness, untimely death, and obsession. Given his troubled life, many critics have interpreted his deranged narrators, including the speaker in "The Raven," as reflections of the author's own tortured state of mind. However, Poe was a brilliant and controlled stylist, whose theories of art championed rigorous structure,
40 careful use of language, and the masterful creation of a single, calculated effect. In summary, Poe's fascination with the macabre, equaled by his interest in beauty and logic, exemplify the deeper divisions of the self and its shadowy side: the conflict of beautiful ideals with the darker impulses of human nature.

Am I on Track?

Actual Time Spent Reading

The Raven

**by Edgar Allan Poe from *Complete Tales and Poems*,
pages 773–776. Edison, NJ: Castle Books, 2002.**

Once upon a midnight dreary, while I pondered, weak and weary,
Over many a quaint and curious volume of forgotten lore—
While I nodded, nearly napping, suddenly there came a tapping,
As of someone gently rapping, rapping at my chamber door—
5 "'Tis some visitor," I muttered, "tapping at my chamber door—
      Only this and nothing more."

Ah, distinctly I remember it was in the bleak December;
And each separate dying ember wrought its ghost upon the floor.
Eagerly I wished the morrow;—vainly I had sought to borrow
10 From my books surcease of sorrow—sorrow for the lost Lenore—
For the rare and radiant maiden whom the angels name Lenore—
      Nameless *here* for evermore.

And the silken, sad, uncertain rustling of each purple curtain
Thrilled me—filled me with fantastic terrors never felt before;
15 So that now, to still the beating of my heart, I stood repeating
"'Tis some visitor entreating entrance at my chamber door—
Some late visitor entreating entrance at my chamber door;—
      This it is and nothing more."

Presently my soul grew stronger; hesitating then no longer,
20 "Sir," said I, "or Madam, truly your forgiveness I implore;
But the fact is I was napping, and so gently you came rapping,
And so faintly you came tapping, tapping at my chamber door,
That I scarce was sure I heard you"—here I opened wide the door;—
      Darkness there and nothing more.

25 Deep into that darkness peering, long I stood there wondering, fearing,
Doubting, dreaming dreams no mortal ever dared to dream before;
But the silence was unbroken, and the stillness gave no token,
And the only word there spoken was the whispered word, "Lenore?"
This I whispered, and an echo murmured back the word, "Lenore!"
30   Merely this and nothing more.

Back into the chamber turning, all my soul within me burning,
Soon again I heard a tapping somewhat louder than before.
"Surely," said I, "surely that is something at my window lattice;
Let me see, then, what thereat is, and this mystery explore—
35 Let my heart be still a moment and this mystery explore;—
        'Tis the wind and nothing more!"

Open here I flung the shutter, when, with many a flirt and flutter,
In there stepped a stately Raven of the saintly days of yore;
Not the least obeisance made he; not a minute stopped or stayed he;
40 But, with mien of lord or lady, perched above my chamber door—
Perched upon a bust of Pallas° just above my chamber door—
        Perched, and sat, and nothing more.

Then this ebony bird beguiling my sad fancy into smiling,
By the grave and stern decorum of the countenance it wore,
45 "Though thy crest be shorn and shaven, thou," I said, "art sure no craven,
Ghastly grim and ancient Raven wandering from the Nightly shore—
Tell me what thy lordly name is on the Night's Plutonian shore!"
        Quoth the Raven "Nevermore."

Much I marveled this ungainly fowl to hear discourse so plainly,
50 Though its answer little meaning—little relevancy bore;
For we cannot help agreeing that no living human being
Ever yet was blessed with seeing bird above his chamber door—
Bird or beast upon the sculptured bust above his chamber door,
        With such name as "Nevermore."

55 But the Raven, sitting lonely on the placid bust, spoke only
That one word, as if his soul in that one word he did outpour.
Nothing farther then he uttered—not a feather then he fluttered—
Till I scarcely more than muttered "Other friends have flown before—
On the morrow *he* will leave me, as my Hopes have flown before."
60   Then the bird said "Nevermore."

_____

41. Pallas: Pallas Athena, the Greek goddess of wisdom.

Startled at the stillness broken by reply so aptly spoken,
"Doubtless," said I, "what it utters is its only stock and store
Caught from some unhappy master whom unmerciful Disaster
Followed fast and followed faster till his songs one burden bore—
65   Till the dirges of his Hope that melancholy burden bore
      Of 'Never—nevermore.'"

But the Raven still beguiling my sad fancy into smiling,
Straight I wheeled a cushioned seat in front of bird, and bust and door;
Then, upon the velvet sinking, I betook myself to linking
70   Fancy unto fancy, thinking what this ominous bird of yore—
  What this grim, ungainly, ghastly, gaunt, and ominous bird of yore
      Meant in croaking "Nevermore."

This I sat engaged in guessing, but no syllable expressing
To the fowl whose fiery eyes now burned into my bosom's core;
75   This and more I sat divining, with my head at ease reclining
On the cushion's velvet lining that the lamplight gloated o'er,
But whose velvet-violet lining with the lamplight gloating o'er,
      She shall press, ah, nevermore!

Then, methought, the air grew denser, perfumed from an unseen censer
80   Swung by seraphim° whose footfalls tinkled on the tufted floor.
"Wretch," I cried, "thy God hath lent thee—by these angels he hath sent
    thee
Respite—respite and nepenthe° from thy memories of Lenore;
Quaff, oh quaff this kind nepenthe and forget this lost Lenore!"
      Quoth the Raven "Nevermore."

85   "Prophet!" said I, "thing of evil!—prophet still, if bird or devil!
Whether Tempter sent, or whether tempest tossed thee here ashore,
Desolate yet all undaunted, on this desert land enchanted—
On this home by Horror haunted—tell me truly, I implore—
Is there—*is* there balm in Gilead?°—tell me—tell me, I implore!"
90   Quoth the Raven "Nevermore."

---

80. seraphim: the highest of the nine ranks of angels.
82. nepenthe: a sleeping potion which people long ago believed would relieve pain and sorrow.
89. Is there . . . balm in Gilead?: a line from the Bible meaning *Is there any relief from my sorrow?*

"Prophet!" said I, "thing of evil!—prophet still, if bird or devil!
By that Heaven that bends above us—by that God we both adore—
Tell this soul with sorrow laden if, within the distant Aidenn,
It shall clasp a sainted maiden whom the angels name Lenore—
95   Clasp a rare and radiant maiden whom the angels name Lenore."
        Quoth the Raven "Nevermore."

"Be that word our sign of parting, bird or fiend!" I shrieked,
    upstarting—
"Get thee back into the tempest and the Night's Plutonian shore!
Leave no black plume as a token of that lie thy soul hath spoken!
100   Leave my loneliness unbroken!—quit the bust above my door!
Take thy beak from out my heart, and take thy form from off my
    door!"
        Quoth the Raven "Nevermore."

And the Raven, never flitting, still is sitting, *still* is sitting
On the pallid bust of Pallas just above my chamber door;
105   And his eyes have all the seeming of a demon's that is dreaming,
And the lamplight o'er him streaming throws his shadow on the
    floor;
And my soul from out that shadow that lies floating on the floor
    Shall be lifted—nevermore!

Am I on Track?

Actual Time Spent Reading

Poe's Process:
Writing "The Raven"

by Sofia Arella, from eapoe.com. The POEtry Society, 27 May 2006.

Many years ago, after the hugely successful publication of "The Raven," Poe wrote an essay describing how he composed it. He described the writing of the poem as though he were solving a mathematical puzzle. Here are some of the first steps in Poe's writing process:

1. He decided he wanted to write a poem with a melancholy° effect.

2. Then he decided that the melancholy would be reinforced by the refrain "Nevermore" (he liked its sound) and that a raven would utter the refrain. (Before he settled on a raven, though, he considered other birds for the part.)

3. Finally, he decided his subject would be what he thought was the most melancholy subject in the world: a lover mourning for a beautiful woman who has died.

Now Poe was ready to write. The first stanza he wrote, he claimed, was the climactic one, lines 85–90. From there he set about choosing his details: the interior space in which the lover, who is a student, and the raven are brought together; the tapping that introduces the raven; the fact that the night is stormy rather than calm; and the action of the raven alighting on the bust of Pallas.

Then Poe goes on to describe his writing process:

"The raven addressed, answers with its customary word, 'Nevermore'—a word which finds immediate echo in the melancholy heart of the student, who, giving utterance aloud to certain thoughts suggested by the occasion, is again startled by the fowl's repetition of 'Nevermore.'

6. **melancholy:** sad or gloomy, e.g., My friend lead a **melancholy** life for many months after losing her father to cancer.

NOTES

"The student now guesses the state of the case, but is impelled, as I have before explained, by the human thirst for self-torture, and in part by superstition, to propound such queries to the bird as will

30 bring him, the lover, the most of the luxury of sorrow, through the anticipated answer 'Nevermore.' . . .

"It will be observed that the words 'from out my heart' involve the first metaphorical expression in the poem. They, with the answer 'Nevermore,' dispose the mind to seek a moral in all that has been previously narrated. The reader begins now to regard the raven as emblematical [symbolic]—but it is not until the very last line of the very last stanza, that the intention of making him emblematical of *Mournful and never ending Remembrance* is permitted distinctly to be seen. . . ."

Am I on Track?

Actual Time Spent Reading

Prose Constructed-Response

Complete the following prose-constructed response that will be scored. You may refer to your reading notes, and you should cite text evidence in your response. You will be able to refer to your response as you write your essay in Part 2.

Prose Constructed-Response Write a paragraph explaining how "The Raven" displays Poe's interest in the "dark, irrational depths of the human mind."

_____

_____

_____

_____

_____

_____

_____

_____

_____

_____

_____

_____

_____

_____

_____

_____

_____

▶ Part 2 (85 minutes)

You now have 85 minutes to review your notes and sources and to plan, draft, revise, and edit your essay. While you may use your notes and refer to the sources, your essay must represent your original work. Now read your assignment and begin your work.

Your assignment

You have read three texts by or about Edgar Allan Poe.

• "Edgar Allan Poe"

• "The Raven"

• "Poe's Process: Writing 'The Raven'"

Write a literary analysis of "The Raven," explaining how the poem explains the "human thirst for self-torture" as Poe himself proclaimed.

Develop your essay by citing evidence from both texts. Be sure to follow the conventions of standard English.

Now begin work on your essay. Manage your time carefully so that you can:

1. plan your essay

2. write your essay

3. revise and edit your final draft

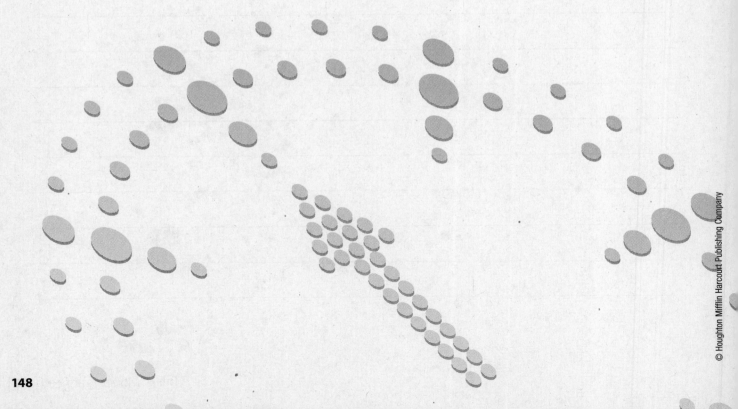

Acknowledgments

"REXANO Proves Politicians and Lobbyists Introducing and Passing Laws Against Exotic Animal Ownership in the Name of 'Public Safety' Use False and Misleading Claims" from *PRWeb,* March 17, 2007, www. prweb.com. Text copyright © 2007 by Rexano. Reprinted by permission of Rexano.

"Social Media, Pretend Friends, and the Lie of False Intimacy" by Jay Baer from *Convince & Convert,* www.convinceandconvert.com. Text copyright © 2008-2013 by Convince & Convert, LLC. Reprinted by permission of Convince & Convert, LLC.

"Spring is like a perhaps hand" from *Complete Poems: 1904–1962* by E. E. Cummings. Text copyright © 1923, 1925, 1951, 1953, 1991 by the Trustees for the E. E. Cummings Trust. Text copyright © 1976 by George James Firmage. Reprinted by permission of Liveright Publishing Corporation.

"Study: The Internet Helps You Make More Friends, Be More Social" by Graeme McMillan from *Time,* June 16, 2011, www.techland.time.com. Text copyright © 2011 by Time, Inc. Reprinted by permission of Time, Inc.